The Fraud Prevention (FP)101 Handbook

An Illustrated Guide to Consumer Fraud Awareness

by
David Tracey
Author of *The Mortgage Handbook*
and Creator of FP101.net

DEDICATION

For Mark, Phillip & Frank.

TABLE OF CONTENTS

NOTABLE ANTI-FRAUD QUOTES

"Our ability to manufacture fraud now exceeds our ability to detect it".
— AL PACINO - A MAN OF MANY PARTS.

"The opposite of knowledge is not ignorance, but deceit and fraud".
— JEAN BAUDRILLARD - FRENCH SOCIOLOGIST & PHILOSOPHER

"The first and worst of all frauds is to cheat one's self. All sin is easy after that".
— PEARL BAILEY - SINGER & ACTRESS

"The history of government management of money has, except for a few short happy periods, been one of incessant fraud and deception".
— FRIEDRICH AUGUST VON HAYEK - ECONOMIST & PHILOSOPHER.

"The fraudster's greatest liability is the certainty that the fraud is too clever to be detected".
— LOUIS J. FREEH - EX FBI DIRECTOR.

Author's Foreword

Hello and welcome.

The first, and most important, thing to know about fraud is that you are probably already a victim. Little doubt about it. By the time you finish this handbook, you will know how, where, and when it happened. So, you are in the right place if you want to protect yourself from the fraud frenzy we now live with.

"It's never just any one thing with fraud."

Fraud is a dense and endless topic. Sure, there are many definitions of what fraud is in the media. It's covered daily in the news, TV shows, books, and movies. Usually in these cases, the good and bad guys are clearly defined for us. Unfortunately, real fraud crime is not so easy to identify until after the reveal. Modern fraud is variable, limitless, and easily penetrates all cultures to the point of being in plain sight. Many people don't recognize it because so many of these schemes have been around for so long. Scams that have stood the test of time are often regarded as legitimate. This is a mix of deception and trickery.

FRAUD

There are many who see fraud and deception as a byproduct of creative genius—that's us! An inspirational human trait of sorts. That might be true if we had any control over it. But we don't. Survivors of a fraud event don't have the luxury of entertaining anything admirable about it. Make no mistake here; deceit is always the tool of choice with fraud. Thus, its bad ethics are without doubt.

When it comes to spreading misery, fraud does not discriminate. It sees no color, creed, or class. No one is immune. The most you can do about fraud is to prepare for the worst and hope for the best. Above all, you must stay optimistic and learn to handle the subject honestly and efficiently. That's where this book comes in.

We'll be covering a lot of content as fraud is a vast topic. But don't worry. It's not about remembering every little detail. Effective learning is about seeing the bigger picture and relating it to your life. You will be equipped with the tools to protect yourself and be much better able to spot a fraud event before it hits you.

What you learn in this book (and course!) might make you realize that you have been or are currently being defrauded. If this happens, know that you are not alone. It is okay. We will show you what you need to do if you find yourself trapped in the web of a fraud event. Better still, you will be fraud aware and know exactly what you need to do to protect your family and friends from fraud and its ugly consequences.

This book is intended to be not just an education, it is also a guided tour of fraud as an urgent topic. So, pay attention and you will become fraud aware. Education is prevention. It is the only real cure for the fraud frenzy we now live in.

Chapter 1

THE FRAUD PREVENTION (FP) BASICS

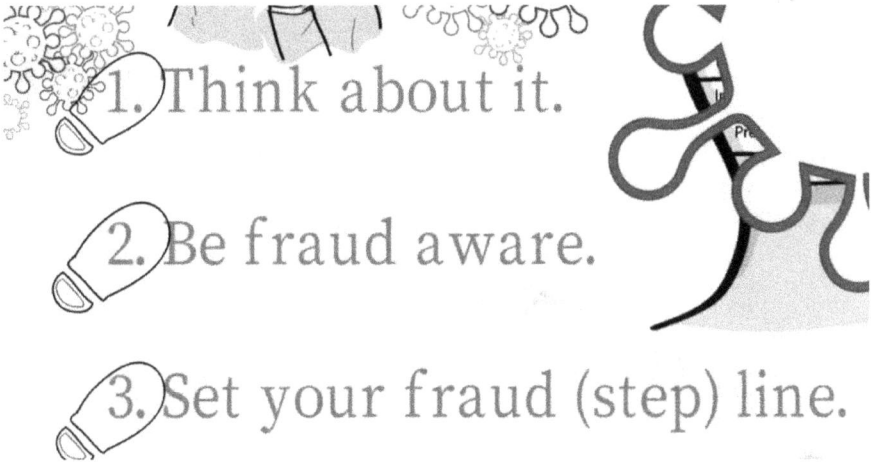

1. Think about it.

2. Be fraud aware.

3. Set your fraud (step) line.

The three key steps for your personal fraud protection are:

1. Think about it.

You have already taken this first step by being here. You must think about fraud prevention to beat fraud. Education is prevention.

2. Be fraud aware!

The key to victory in any battle is to know your enemy. That means you have to know what fraud is; you will know it by its ugly consequences which are usually many. According to our early research results, less than 50 percent of folks living in the developed world know what fraud is and even fewer know how it functions.

3. Have a fraud (step) line.

This is a priority. If you are fraud aware, you will already have a (step) line. This is your most powerful fraud prevention tool. You probably use it already, we're just here to sharpen it up for you! Your (step) line is a serious and subjective topic which we will come back to shortly.

What is fraud?—a few definitions.

To know what fraud is, you first have to realize it. And that's not easy. You have to know your enemy, not understand it. At least 50 percent of people do NOT know what fraud really is, so we need to get a handle on it. That's why we're here! Let's do that right now.

Fraud is…

…a one-word cliché that divides and conquers all before it. It's part of a keenly developed survival instinct. Welcome to the top of the food chain! It's rarely just one thing. It's usually a load of moving parts—pervasive, cunning, and emotive. A mental jigsaw puzzle, rarely physical. It's something that plays games with numbers—such is its power! An opportunist in times of change or in a crisis. An exploitation of any vulnerability in all circumstances. It destroys a large percentage of its victims. Some people just can't move past a fraud event.

The vast majority of fraud crimes go unreported and the number we're discussing here is 95 percent. This is what makes fraud the *crime of choice* and an opportunity for career criminals. It's a cost to humanity of *trillions* of dollars every year. This is the real enemy of all humanity. We could spend the rest of our time here rolling out fraud descriptions, but we've got a lot of ground to cover. So, let's keep it short.

FRAUD IS…
THEFT BY DECEPTION!

Chapter 2

A CLINICAL ANATOMY OF FRAUD
(THE FRAUD DIAMOND)

The fraud diamond started out as criminologist Donald Cressey's "The Fraud Triangle" published in 1953 in the book, *Other People's Money: A Study in the Social Psychology of Embezzlement* (OPM). Over the next fifty years, the fraud diamond theory evolved out of this and was published in December 2004 by Wolfe and Hermanson. The fraud diamond is an expanded version of the fraud triangle.

These concepts are used as essential tools to help understand the basic elements of fraud events. The difference between the fraud triangle and the fraud diamond is the addition of *capability* as another essential element of the fraud anatomy.

Please note that the fraud diamond theory is mostly used in the area of occupational fraud analysis. That does not stop it from being a very useful fraud prevention tool for anyone who takes the time to understand the structure of the fraud events it demonstrates.

1. Pressure, incentive
and motivation.

2. Opportunity.

4. Capability.

3. Rationale.

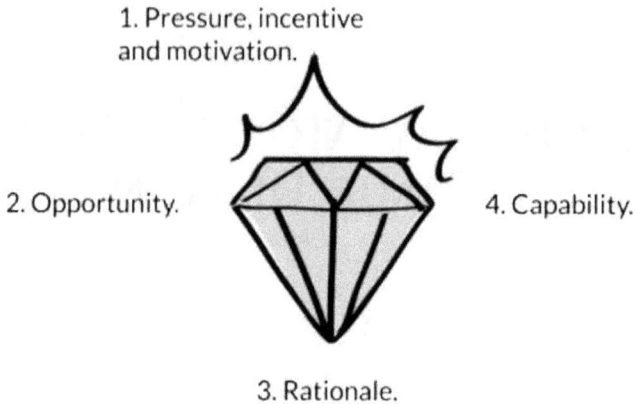

The Fraud Diamond has four headings:

1. **Pressure, incentive, and motivation.**

2. **Opportunity.**

3. **Rationale.**

4. **Capability.**

1. Perceived pressures.

Perpetraitors (that's how WE spell it) come under perceived pressure which leads to their unethical behavior. The word "perceived" is important in this context because often the pressure is non-existent. Yes, there are many people who get up every morning and create angst to swing out of. The most common sources of these pressures are:

A. **Financial.** The most common motive.

B. **Job related.**

C. **External or third-party pressure.** This includes compromised persons.

Types of "perceived" pressures include greed, consumer addictions, expenses and personal debt, family problems or health, and even just resentment. We must include drug addiction and gambling in this toxic mix, too. These kinds of perceived pressures are often just a step away from an obsession with material gain. Such self-induced stresses create motive and incentive.

2. Perceived Opportunity.

This is always the unlocked door to fraud. If perpetraitors don't get presented with opportunities, they cannot commit their crimes. Fraud opportunities are usually created by poor controls and lack of supervision. Accounting professionals have loads of theories about this stuff. Ask and they'll happily sing it for you.

3. Rationalization.

Most perpetraitors have created a morally acceptable justification for committing their frauds. Without it, fraud crime events would drop quickly. Rationale examples include, "I am only borrowing the money," "I am entitled to this money," or "I have to provide for my family," "My employers are cheating me," and so on. Besides entitlement and resentment, hate and prejudice are also added to this mix.

Rationalization is very difficult to spot because it's often buried within an ideology. Whatever the reason, any fraud is unethical and can always be traced back to flawed values and a weak character. Thus, some bizarre rationale will emerge.

4. Capability.

This is about having the necessary traits, skills, and abilities to commit fraud. It is about seeing a specific opportunity and acting on it. Ego, knowledge, cleverness, position, intelligence, deceit, anger, coercion, and stress are all factors in a fraud capability. Then comes the debate about whether committing fraud is another type of psychopathic behavior when it comes to mass fraud. More on this later.

So now we have narrowed the fraud description all the way down to one word. Theft. Specifically, theft of money and all the forms it takes in our age of material wealth. So how do they do that?

Chapter 3

THE ANATOMY OF A
FRAUD PERPETRAITOR

Remember, it's never any one thing with fraud; it's usually a few things happening all at once. It takes a keen power of observation to spot a fraud perpetraitor on the job. A combination of at least a few of these characteristics are in all fraudsters. For your own sake, do not rush to judgement. We have limited this to nine personal traits used by fraud perpetraitors tactically.

1. Charming and tactile.

This is the kind of person you are more than happy to bring home to meet your folks. In fact, this person is so charismatic, you start introducing them around to your friends immediately after you meet!

2. Narcissistic.

You have to be sharp to spot this trait early. It is usually very well hidden. Fraudsters are usually self-aware people.

3. Egocentric.

We're all a bit of this! Face in a crowd? Perpetraitors amp this one up. Often used as a diversion during the fraud process. It's often called, "the distraction lie." Ego plays a lead role in most fraud events.

4. Committed and motivated.

This is a creative way of diverting the mark (the targeted person) from the reality. Again, the distraction lie is very much at play here. A common method used to trigger empathy with the mark!

5. Aloof or separate in a group.

Fraud perpetraitors are criminals who view the world differently from the rest of us. This social fracture disposition is part of the fraud dichotomy.

6. Nothing to lose but their time.

Professional criminals have a cliché, "If you can't do the time, don't commit the crime." Most fraudsters do it for the lifestyle. The thrill of the chase. The power over others. There's always an extra risk in trusting someone with nothing to lose.

7. Materially driven and consumer oriented.

Perpetraitors are tuned into all the ways of spending money fast. Consumer goods and gadgets are a favorite. Be wary of those who talk non-stop about what they want to spend their money on.

8. Controlling.

They will go to great lengths to control their immediate environs, especially when and where their game is on. For long plays, vacations and sick days happen rarely because of the risk of exposure. Many long and expensive frauds only come to light because of an unplanned absence by the perpetraitor.

9. An occasionally psychotic psychopath.

Often the stress gets to them and they get into a meltdown. Rarely violent, but it has happened. With low level street frauds, violence is usually imminent. Your money is gone.

Note of CAUTION: These are just guidelines. Having this information does not make anyone judge and jury, especially you. A false accusation can be detrimental to everybody. The use and interpretation of these signs should be used to initiate a closer investigation. Either get the evidence or step away if that's an option. It's all about your fraud line. You won't be remembered for the battles you lose.

Money comes easily to an accomplished fraudster. It goes even quicker. That's why your money is already gone. Easy come, easy go, and go easy (on you).

THE PERPETRAITOR'S ANATOMY OF A FRAUD EVENT

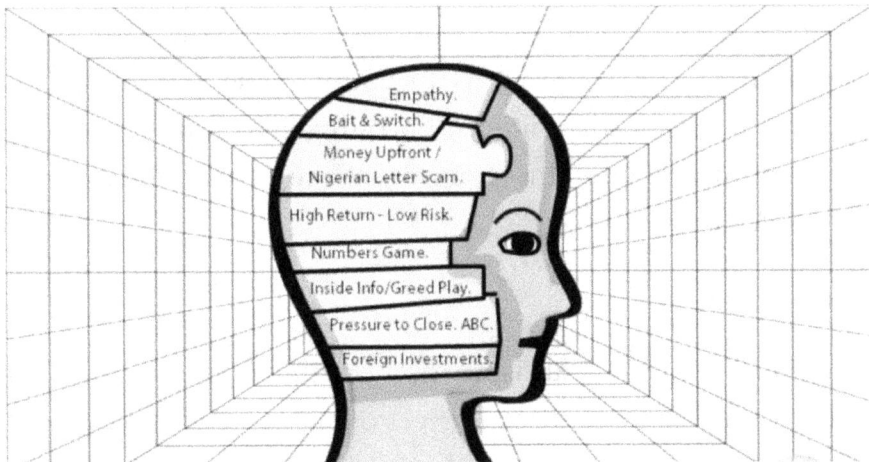

Empathy.
Bait & Switch.
Money Upfront /
Nigerian Letter Scam.
High Return - Low Risk.
Numbers Game.
Inside Info/Greed Play.
Pressure to Close. ABC.
Foreign Investments.

"It's rarely any one thing with fraud, it's usually a series of events with a reveal at the end. But better than a movie or a book · this is real and then your money is..G·O·N·E!"
·Dapper Dan.

1. Access data.

The perpetraitor must gain access to the data that will enable the crime. This will be your date of birth, email address, social security number, home address, any personal phone number or utility bill. Any of these items grant easy access to almost anyone's data and personal history. All the info enabling frauds will always be traced back as having come from the victim.

2. Engage the victim.

The second need is to engage with the target. Remotely or in person. It doesn't matter. First contact is used to build credibility and empathize with the mark. Empathy will then be sustained whenever and wherever possible at this point. The initial approach of any fraudster is to endorse and encourage the victim's beliefs and ambitions. Encouragement and agreement are very strong empathy triggers. We're even programming robots/AI to do this.

3. Get past security.

The third requirement is to get through any diligence or background check and to have you let your guard down. Many frauds stumble and fail here but many more get through on the basis of people feeling uncomfortable with running a background check on someone new in their lives. They view it as disrespectful. No, it is not! It's just an excuse not to do it. Running a background check takes more time and effort than what it costs. This is not only a serious personal security issue; it is also part of your wealth nurturing process. Liking someone is not a background check. Start with backgroundcheck.org. It's the least you should do before trusting anyone.

4. Create confusion.

The fourth requirement is to create a reason to change the deal after a commitment is made. Deals change all the time. They are living entities until they are done. Some people see the signing of contract as the start of negotiations, not the finish. "The devil is in the details." Fraudsters thrive on confusion and fast change. Delegate these decisions at your own risk. Deal changes are a red flag for fraud.

This is a moment of *onus*. Hold on to that word and we will come back to it later.

5. Cause lots of collateral damage.

The fifth and most ugly—fraud events rarely end with just a material loss. Most fraudsters work hard at creating as much confusion and collateral damage when their scam is revealed or exposed. They will pursue any exit even after the key turns in the prison door behind them. The fallout from a fraud can often be a lot uglier and much costlier than the main event itself. Even a victim can lose their reputation after a fraud event. Another reason they do not report it.

Fraud has many facets and is often presented as a diamond of human skill and genius in movies and modern books, especially spy stories for example. Maybe lies and betrayal are creative processes, but the collateral damage from any fraud event puts it firmly in the dark space of human nature.

For example, when charities get hit by a fraud event, they suffer a severe collapse with donations. Clarity and honesty mean little in dealing with such a sad and ugly matter. So, they have to take multiple losses. Often accused of being too trusting, a lot of charities believe trusting folks is where their work begins. That's just one reason why they are besieged by fraudsters. The only thing a fraud perpetraitor really sees is vulnerability. Your weakness is their opportunity.

Chapter 5

ANATOMY OF FRAUD—
CONSEQUENCES

This is not something people usually pay much attention to. For your information, it's too late to become outraged after the fact. The epicenter of a fraud is one thing. The ripples coming out of it can be like a tidal wave upon our lives. Some consequences of fraud include:

1. A huge sense of loss and betrayal.

Emotional reactions on several levels. This speaks for itself. The average cost of a fraud event to a business is over 100K plus time, disruption, material cost, and heartache.

2. Collateral damage.

It's never any one thing with fraud; it's usually a combination. The true situation typically becomes clear only sometime after the event. Even in the small frauds. In the US savings and loan fraud, it took twelve years to figure it all out and add up the cost. Perpetraitors will go to great lengths to cause as much disruption as they can in their fraud environment. Planned, deliberate, and very effective.

3. Law enforcement reaction variations.

Law enforcement's experience with fraud matters and crime generally does not allow them the luxury of anything less than skepticism when dealing with this subject. So, if you're expecting sympathy or flashing blue lights, you are surely in the wrong place.

4. The fraud stigma.

People will not get involved in a fraud dispute. Fraud is like the plague. Most people really don't want to hear *anything* about it—not even for their personal protection. The end.

5. Mitigation.

Don't have any expectations. Your money is gone. A huge proportion of victims immediately saddle up in hot pursuit of their property after a fraud event. After committing a lot of time, money, and effort on recovery and mitigation they find that their money is gone. The percentage of people who recover anything afterwards is very low.

6. Investigations vs resources.
Fraud and the legal system.

It comes as a huge shock to many people when they discover what a low priority fraud events have with law enforcement professionals, including the judiciary. They keep a very simple view of it. Murder, rape, personal violence and their prevention are top priorities. Sure, fraud crime is a priority, too! The main challenge with fraud is evidence. Fraud is tough to prove. The victim needs hard evidence. The perpetraitor only needs deniability and a good lawyer. It's one of the main reasons why so much fraud crime goes unreported.

7. Who said what, where, when, and how?

Ultimately, most fraud crimes come down to a personal dispute. One person's word against the other. That brings us back to our first rule. Prevention through education is the only real cure for fraud.

8. Your HBU—highest and best use—of a fraud event.

If you ever have the misfortune of finding yourself caught up in a fraud event, there are only two options: *learn from it* and *step away from it*. That's what the smart people do. You're not supposed to like it.

Chapter 6

Your Fraud (Step) Line

Any fraud prevention mindset requires a (step) line. Your fraud (step) line is a subjective and rhetorical topic. This means we are not here to preach morality, religion, politics, or officially give you any financial advice.

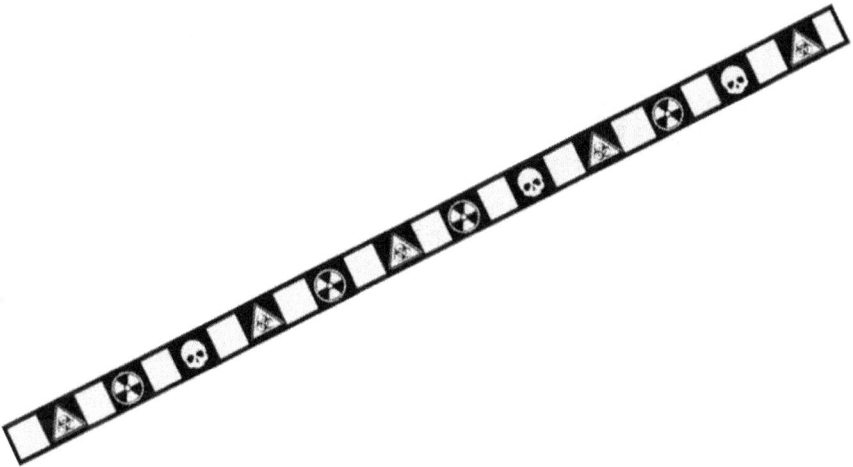

This may well be the most important issue that we will cover in this resource. When you have read this, you will have a much clearer idea of where to draw your line on fraud. This is your (step) line—where you will step aside because you can or cannot see what's coming. This can only be your decision. No one can make it for you. Not even if you are wealthy, privileged, and extremely lucky. In this day and age, fraud and deceit are everywhere. Any person should choose very carefully what they believe or embrace.

The language—fraud vs rip-off and media apologists.

You must understand the language of modern fraud. It's not real. Here are two examples that explain the situation:

If something is a fraud, you are obliged, as the good citizen that you are, to report it to the police. In a professional or business situation, it is strict practice to follow a process including a police report and complaint. Being ripped off is an entirely different matter. If you've been ripped off, it means the thief is gone with the loot. It means you made a bad decision, business or otherwise. The responsibility is yours. So, while fraud and rip-off are the exact same thing, in one situation you follow a procedure and in the other, you just quit—there and then.

The point is, fraud is a crime, getting ripped off isn't. This is part of the sanitation process. Because something is called a "rip-off" does not mean it's not a fraud. It just means you aren't going to do anything about it.

The second example is a subject up soon on our topics. The Ponzi scheme versus mass fraud. In a short research sampling, over 50 percent of people surveyed did not know that both were the same thing. Which sounds more real? Ponzi or mass fraud? This is how you are being distanced from the reality of fraud. As soon as you call it mass fraud instead of Ponzi, the fraud crime landscape changes considerably.

Humanity is felonious. Over 70 percent of people are opportunistic thieves.

In a recent advanced research study, a vending machine was set up to refund people their money after they received their purchases. There was a service number for technical help across the top of the machine, big and bold. No one called the vending machine company. In fact, many folks called their friends to tell them about the "faulty" machine. This is our reality.

The onus; placing responsibility.
The mouse and the peanut butter.

Dapper Dan's Real Peanut Butter

If you put a mouse within sniffing distance of a glob of peanut butter, it will go crazy to get at it. Theft does not come into it. So, by placing the peanut butter where the mouse can get it, the onus is placed on the mouse. Or is it? Who is responsible for the peanut butter? The mouse or the person who gave it access? By placing the onus on someone else for our material interests does not mean it's a safe thing to do.

For example, our banking systems (aka Wall Street) provide essential services and a mutual trust empowers those services on both sides. Sad to tell, in recent years that trust has collapsed, especially with our youngest generation. There are very few, if any financial institutions who have not been heavily penalized for systemic breaches of trust in the last twenty years. This is the key reason why our global financial system is slowly collapsing. Whatever comes out of this collapse will take trust out of all financial transactions. It'll be like putting the lid back on your peanut butter.

Setting your fraud (step) line. Trust follows empathy.

The key element of all fraud is the misplacement of trust. The first step in gaining trust with another person is by using empathy. Empathy is defined as the sharing of an emotion between two or more people. Fraudsters do this very well in the glibbest way possible. Your empathy is your first and last line of defense against fraud. Empathy and trust are like Siamese twins and just as hard to separate. So, protect your empathy. It is who you are and where you live!

Good paperwork is an enemy of fraud.

Fraud perpetraitors get very wary of people who do their paperwork. This is the one who emails a summary after a meeting, hitting the main points of a recent chat or proposed deal. This goes a long way to disrupting fraudulent activity and "mistakes." It is also the quickest way to identify fraud activities. They just hate it. So, you should remember what you learned about paperwork during potty training?

"The job is not finished until the paperwork is done!"

Poor business decisions.

There is also a fine line between fraud and a bad business decision. A bad decision comes from poor judgement. All a fraudster needs are deniability and a sharp lawyer to walk away from the most heinous of financial crimes. So, a bad business decision usually stems from lack of attention to detail before getting into something.

In the case of investors and diligence, there are three key rules. Verify, verify, and, oh yeah...verify! Ultimately, and sad to say, many people perceive fraud victims as having made a bad business decision. They might have a point, so think about this before calling fraud!

Setting your fraud (step) line.

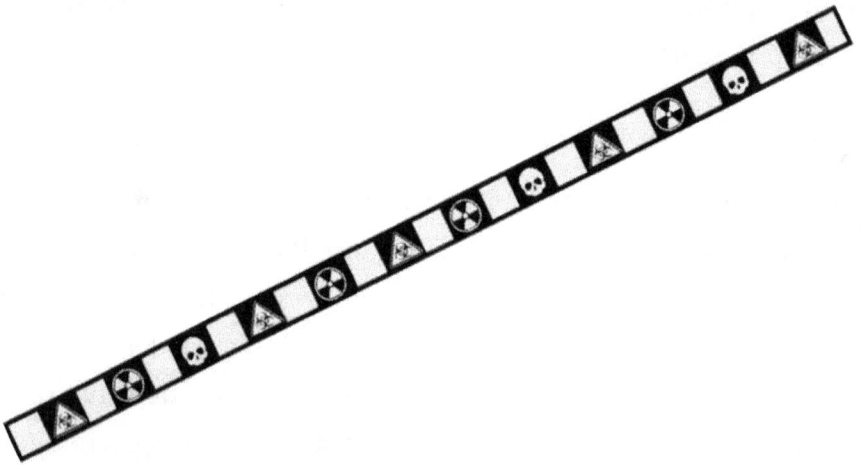

Everybody must have one. Once you reach that line, you make the call. If you don't or won't, then you're done—in more ways than one—because it's never just one thing with a fraud.

Chapter 7

THE MILESTONES TO OUR FRAUD FRENZY

Roman Empire—title fraud.

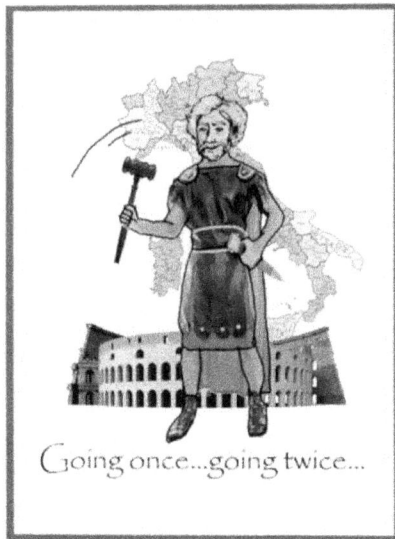

Going once...going twice...

193 A.D.: The Praetorian Guard murdered the Emperor and sold the Roman Empire to the highest bidder. There were fraud issues for the Romans, Greeks, Persians, Egyptians, and so on. So, technically there's nothing new under the sun when it comes to fraud except for the level of fraud that we are seeing in the

world now. However, this Roman Empire deal did not hold up. Someone needs to tell the Americans.

The John Law bank fraud.

1720: John Law and the Mississippi Land Bubble. This one set France on fire. John Law (1671 – 1729) was a Scottish economist who found favor at the court of Louis XV and effectively set up the first central bank on a national scale. This was all to the financial benefit of the French monarchy and France too, of course. Starting with writing off the national debt, Law bankrupted thousands of French investors with a major fraud through his Bank Royale. In 1718, using a novel marketing scheme for its time, Law sold shares via his corporate vehicles known as The Mississippi Company.

Aggressive selling tactics created a huge demand for these shares. So, more and more paper notes were issued until the end of 1720. Then the French government was forced to admit it did not have the coin to back all these notes. Of course, there was an immediate bank run and pop went this property bubble. Law ended his days nine years later as a professional gambler in Venice.

William "520 Percent" Miller.

> Fraud Frenzy
>
> # The Crooklyn Times
>
> ## Major swindler gets conned by a con man

1899: William "520 Percent" Miller opened for business as the "Franklin Syndicate" in Brooklyn, New York. Miller promised ten percent a week in interest and exploited some of the main themes of scalable mass fraud, aka Ponzi schemes. This included customers re-investing the interest they earned. He defrauded his "clients" out of one-million dollars and was sentenced to ten years in jail.

This fraud demonstrates the first recorded use of a modern math-based system for large-scale consumer fraud. Exactly twenty-one years later, Charles Ponzi based his model on Miller's event.

Charles Ponzi.

1920: In Boston, Charles Ponzi introduced a supposed arbitrage scheme which was a masquerade for paying off early investors with the deposits of later investors.

He claimed he would double investors' money in ninety days through a bizarre plan to buy and resell international postal-reply coupons. Over 30,000 investors were ruined in a seven-month timescale. It was the largest reported mass fraud for several generations.

Mass fraud is not just a Ponzi scheme. It's scalable mass fraud. This means that one or a multiple of victims can be stolen from using the same method simultaneously. Using the Ponzi name to describe such mass fraud demonstrates how much we dislike even applying the correct name and description to mass fraud. We allow ourselves to be distracted so easily. Ponzi is not a media cartoon character. He was a sociopath. He really did spread an enormous amount of pain, destruction, and human misery.

None of that matters in the pursuit of a good sound bite. Mathematical schemes for mass fraud are now called Ponzi Schemes and are so named for Charles Ponzi who died alone, broke, and almost blind. Utterly unrepentant, even boastful—like so many fraud recidivists.

Chapter 8

MASS FRAUD 101

How Mass Fraud (aka a Ponzi Scheme) Works.

These are fraudulent investment operations that pay returns to separate investors from their own money or money paid by subsequent investors, rather than from any actual profit earned. Mass fraud schemes are simply ways of "robbing Peter to pay Paul." A modern fraud methodology on steroids. Scalable mass fraud. Extra powerful stuff.

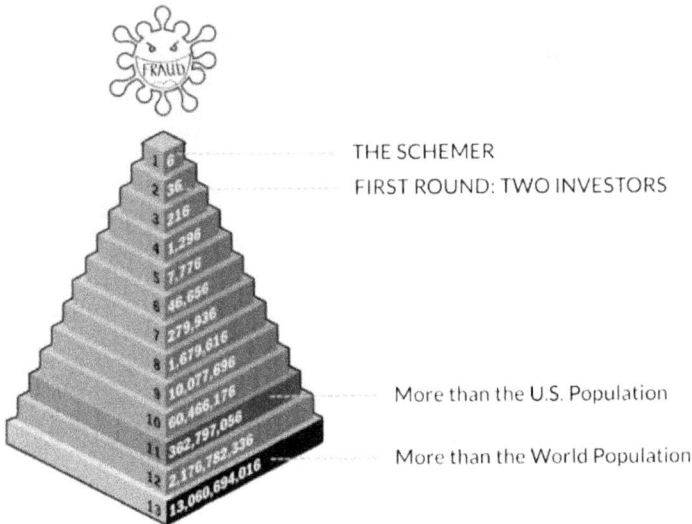

THE SCHEMER
FIRST ROUND: TWO INVESTORS

More than the U.S. Population

More than the World Population

The reason folks keep returning to the Ponzi scheme as a description of scalable mass fraud is because they can assume people know what they're talking about without having to use "boring" explanations. So, Ponzi is a sound bite with its own meaning. Scalable mass frauds, also known as Ponzi schemes, are in reality, a basic and simple fraud scheme empowered by false perceptions and misplaced trust.

If you compare the Ponzi mass fraud scheme to the Madoff fraud, you will see that they are similar frauds in all ways except it's like comparing the wheel to a computer. All mass fraud nowadays is very sophisticated. They use numbers, technology, and marketing as much as they do education and communications to get their message across. However, the best way to explain mass fraud is to take all the numbers out of it. That leaves four short steps for the perpetraitors and eight long, painful ones for the victims.

The Mass Fraud Cycle (in 8 or less) steps.

When you take away the window dressing and static noise, mass fraud methods are not impressive. A basic process is very clear to see.

Step 1: Recruit the first few investors.

This is just like the launch of any new product except for the promoter's intent. In many cases it simply starts out as a good business plan with a great concept. This morphs into a full-blown fraud when the promoters realize how hard they have to work for real success. This is just one reason why it is very hard to spot a fraud in its early stages.

Step 2: Pay great dividends quickly.

Step 2: Pay back all the initial investors well
and on time for their risk.
Hustle for reinvestment and "deeper" relationships.

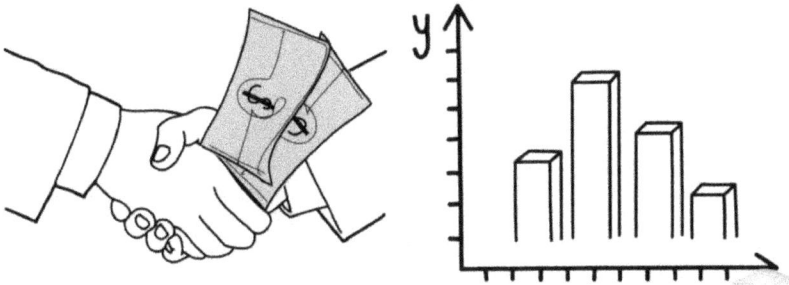

Pay back all the initial investors well and on time for their risk. Hustle for more commitment and "deeper" relationships. This creates a financial track record of "performance and reliability." Shills are commonly used here.

Step 3: Generate a financial history.

Step 3: Use this "track record" with testimonials attached to recruit new investors in a marketing cycle.

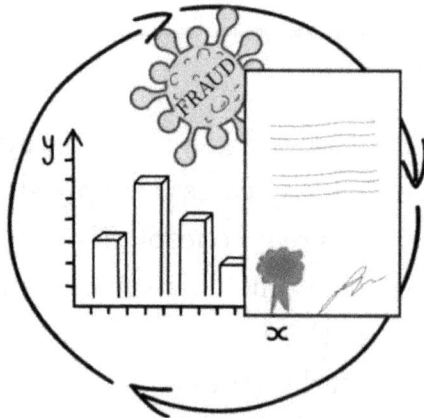

Use this creative "track record" with written testimonials attached to recruit new investors in a marketing cycle. Testimonials and character references are the lifeblood of fraud. Some who provide these are unwitting dupes or enablers, but not always. If it's in print on a glossy brochure it has to be true... right?

Step 4: Rinse and repeat.

Step 4: Rinse and repeat steps 2 & 3
until critical mass is reached.

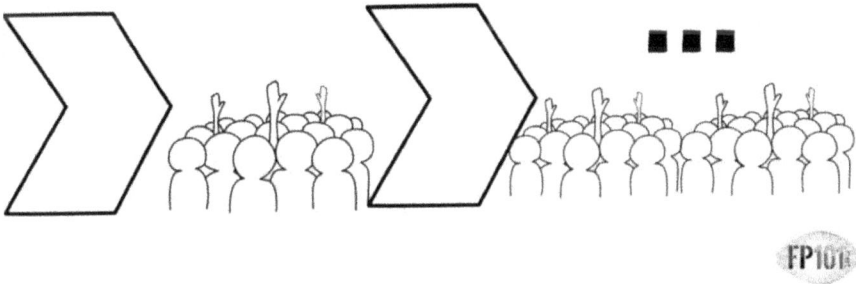

Rinse and repeat steps two and three until a critical mass is reached. This can be done in a matter of weeks these days. A false history, fake referrals and testimonials. Lots of activity. On and on it will go.

Step 5: Critical mass equals crash and burn.

Many media streams treat fraud as a cultural event, others as a "lightweight" filler between adverts.

Many media streams treat fraud as a cultural event, others as a "lightweight" filler between adverts. All fraud schemes collapse. Look around at all the collapsing pension schemes in our world right now. This is institutionally sponsored mass fraud. 1n 1997, the Albanian government collapsed for this very reason.

Step 6: Your money is G-O-N-E!

Step 6: At the point of collapse promotor(s) will usually disappear with anything of value.

At the point of collapse, the promoters will usually disappear with anything of value. All fraudsters have an exit plan, even Madoff, who gave himself up at a time and place of *his* choosing.

Step 7: Mass fraud is now a "regular" business enterprise.

Step 7: For the long frauds, build sustainability and respectability. Use Corporate fronts, $ billions in political lobbying with plenty of brilliant lawyers to create a legitimacy and even some respectability.

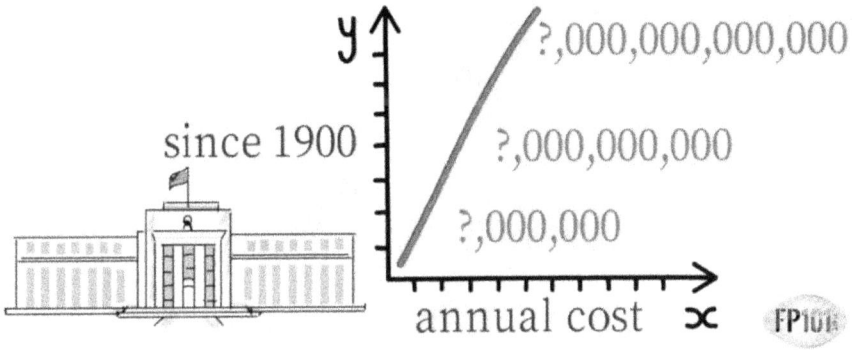

Successful frauds are usually planned and executed with great skill. Mass fraud is a business now. Some of these corporations pay millions in taxes. For a long fraud, they will play the long game. They have corporate fronts with billions of dollars in political lobbying and plenty of brilliant lawyers to create legitimacy and respectability.

Every decade since 1900 has thrown up various mass fraud schemes and so we have gone from millions to billions to trillions for the annual cost of mass fraud. These fraud timelines can last a few days, weeks, or months to decades, even centuries. This mass fraud systemic needs to be seen as a key part of a much larger mass fraud exploitation and comes in many forms.

Step 8: The victim becomes the burden.

For every mass fraud perpetrated, there are thousands of victims. When a fraud scheme collapses, the story usually stops with the victims. Fraud is a great story, victims are not. Who'd willingly want to share their burden?

Chapter 9

SIGNS AND PREVENTION OF MASS FRAUD SYSTEMS

Here are some of the most obvious signs of a possible fraud. It usually comes in several combinations of these perpetraitor strategies.

1. High return for low risk.

If something sounds too good to be true it usually is. We already know this.

2. Unusually consistent and solid returns.

Nobody is that good! Apply the law of averages against everything you are told.

3. Secretive and/or complex strategies.

All good investments have three parts. A beginning, middle, and a good ending. If you don't understand something fully, that is your (step) line. Walk away.

4. Unregistered company or investment.

This is down to your initial due diligence. A bad sign if it is not done properly and correctly. Always know who and what you are dealing with.

5. Paperwork issues.

Documentation might be all you have to show for a bad financial situation. This is within your power to control and handle properly. Remember your potty training! The job is not finished until the paperwork is done!

6. Difficulty getting paid.

Money management issues and debt are definitive red flags that must be investigated before making any commitment. Fraudsters are rarely good money managers.

7. Poor communications.

Usually deliberate. Often used as a tactic. This goes to intent. Money is given, your money is gone.

From Ponzi to Pyramid—it's still (scalable) mass fraud.

The dust had barely settled on the Ponzi event when the world was beset by similar schemes and mass fraud morphed into pyramid selling schemes. All were aimed directly at the middle class, poor, and uneducated alike. Without exception, all pyramid schemes collapse. Between 1920 and 1960, pyramid selling was declared illegal in most developed countries. It's too easy to do and way too profitable to be outlawed and that's why fraud keeps inventing itself.

Chapter 10

CHAIN LETTERS AKA "MAKE MONEY FAST!" ETC.

The David Rhodes Chain

Chain letters or chain mail is illegal in most jurisdictions. It is just another variant of mass fraud. When chain mail works, and it still does, they generate plenty of hard cash. That's why perpetraitors see this fraud as a honey pot for sure. It is interesting to note that the original chain letters were written by popes to distribute prayers to believers.

Now, a chain letter is a personal message that persuades the recipient to make copies and pass them along to either a specific number or as many as the recipient can think up. Again, this is a fraud that exploits not just the target, but the victim's family, friends, and all contacts. It's a classic example of how a fraud looks random, but surely isn't.

Like all mass frauds, the chain letter is an expanding pyramid that cannot sustain itself. These chain letters are written to manipulate and tap into our emotions. They are just another get-rich-quick scheme doomed to fail before it starts. They try to trap our kindness, beliefs, superstitions, and feelings to achieve results, usually for theft of money.

Some of these letters will threaten the recipient with bad luck, physical violence, or even death for anyone who dares to break the chain. Chain letters are still sent by hand delivery, postal service, email messages, social media, bulletin boards, and even text messages.

There are two main types of chain letters: the hoax letter and the Dave Rhodes letter. The *hoax letter* attempts to deceive or defraud recipients. It might be malicious, instructing users to delete an essential computer file by claiming it is a virus. It can also be a scam that persuades users to send money or personal information.

Chain letters as emails have also found a new use in phishing attacks. And we'll cover phishing later. They are also used to generate and sustain false urban legends. Not always written for financial gain, such letters have malice at their core. They are often full of promises or rewards for being forwarded by the recipients.

A classic example of this fraud is what has become known as *The Dave Rhodes chain letter.*

Chain letters are widespread and accepted as part of social media now. Social media boards are awash with them. They're all over YouTube as videos and commentaries. They're easy to find on Facebook through messages or applications.

Chain letters are just everywhere. Often, it can be difficult to see which is genuine or a fraud. Therefore, you need to know how they are structured. To do that, read a few and you will find the same basic structure in all of them.

Why do people think chain letters actually work!?

The reason people are drawn into these schemes is because the average mind does not relate to, wait for it...*geometrical progressions*. Math or geometry intuition is the gift of a very small minority.

Assume that a chain letter has a forwarding list of six people. These folks are promised thousands of letters stuffed with cash from all over the world only if they and their nominees engage fully with the operation. The idea of sending out just a few letters and getting hundreds back stuffed with cash is an offer just too good to be true—and it is.

Yet, people believe it, especially the needy and the greedy. That's most of the population, but still not enough to sustain any mass fraud indefinitely. The numbers necessary to maintain successful rapid growth would soon outstrip the global population. People just don't seem to get this.

All mass fraud schemes are mathematically impossible.

The name at the top of the letter is the one who gets the money. That's how chain letters work. In fact, it would not be unusual for your name, at the bottom, to be the only *real* person there.

Chain letters take many forms, but once you make it your business to understand this framework, you will see it coming. Chain mail peaked in the '50s and '60s before it was made illegal. However, it is now found in a perpetual state of recidivism on the Internet. People still literally buy into it in droves.

Chapter 11

MORE FRAUD MILESTONES

1925: Victor Lustig, fraud recidivist.

In 1925, the Eiffel Tower was sold twice by Victor Lustig and his sidekick, Dapper Dan. This is a guy who took himself very seriously as a professional fraudster. A career criminal, he died in prison while serving a sentence for counterfeiting. His operation was so large at the time of his arrest that it threatened the stability of the US dollar. Victor Lustig is not just remembered for his clever ruse as a count of Eastern European origin, he is also the author of *Rules of the Con*. This, more than anything, shows the utter lack of sincerity and immorality of a fraud perpetraitor.

Victor Lustig's Rules of the Con.

Let's just take a brief look so that we know what makes these fraudsters so utterly toxic.

1. Be a patient listener. For it is this, not fast talking, that gets a con-man his coups.

2. Never look bored.

3. Wait for the other person to reveal any political persuasions, then agree with them.

4. Let the other person reveal religious views, then have the same ones.

5. Hint at sex talk, but don't follow it up unless the other person shows a strong interest.

6. Never discuss illness, unless some special concern is shown.

7. Never pry into a person's personal life. They'll tell you all eventually.

8. Never boast. Just let your importance be quietly obvious.

9. Never be untidy.

10. Never get drunk.

There's nothing random about this list because there is nothing random about any fraud. It's usually very well planned and executed. Just like this list.

FP101.net

Late 50's:
The "quiz show" scandals.

The Daily
FRAUD   Fraud Frenzy

Quiz show frauds force new legislation
Is this legislation too little too late?

Quiz Show

In the late '50s, we had the quiz show scandals. This was the first major media fraud event to become public in the television age. The *$64,000 Question* and *Twenty-One*, two leading US TV quiz shows were revealed as rigged. Winners were chosen and maintained based exclusively on ratings success. Public outrage grew to the point where new legislation was quickly passed.

However, the damage was done, and the cat was out of the bag about fraud. The concept of fraud caught fire in the public imagination and the appetite of villains chasing easy money became fiery.

Money comes easily to an accomplished fraudster. It goes even quicker. That's why your money is already gone.

1959: Amway arrives.

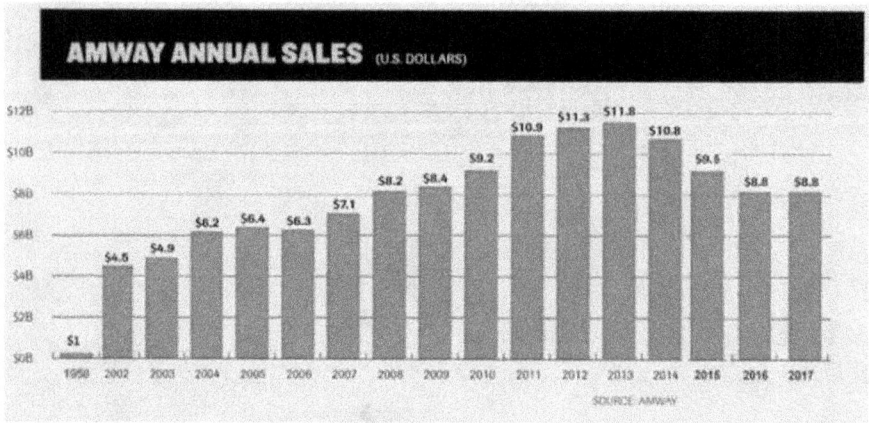

AMWAY ANNUAL SALES (U.S. DOLLARS)

SOURCE: AMWAY

By the early '60s there was a series of events that laid the groundwork for modern mass fraud. It was a convergence of fraud opportunities that created the fraud frenzy we live in now.

1. The rise of mass consumerism and easy credit. Easy come, easy go. Never a truer word said.

2. Amway, the new player in multi-level marketing also known as "direct selling," not only gains a serious foothold with unwitting consumers, it fosters legitimacy through its highly paid and aggressive lawyers and powerful political support. We will explain MLMs and direct selling in more detail shortly.

3. The controversy surrounding major fraud events, such as the quiz show scandals, left folks wondering if everyone was at it. Oh, all those lies, those hypocrites!

4. Events surrounding the Cold War, the Kennedy assassination, the war in Vietnam, Watergate, the war on drugs, and the rise of global terrorism have ripped away any last vestige of innocence the world has. People become even more skeptical and cynical as events unfold. The annual number of fraud events has grown exponentially. We are at the point where the stocks and shares of all major fraud peddlers are traded by Wall Street financiers. The same people who will fund both sides of a war anywhere in the world, the bigger the better.

The Wall Street (fraud) insiders.

1987: Ivan Boesky and Michael Milken, Wall Street insiders.

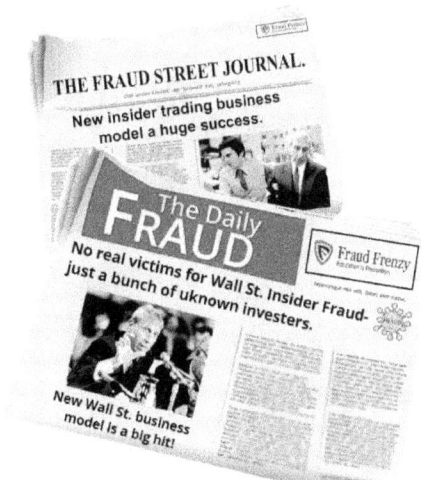

THE FRAUD STREET JOURNAL.

New insider trading business model a huge success.

The Daily FRAUD

No real victims for Wall St. Insider Fraud- just a bunch of uknown investers.

Fraud Frenzy

New Wall St. business model is a big hit!

1987: Ivan Boesky and Michael Milken made history with insider trading. These guys became media heroes when they profited massively from insider trading even after all the penalties were paid. Billions of dollars in profit. Boesky sold out on Milken who now thrives as a philanthropist. Boesky, however, did not do so well.

What makes this fraud standout is that even with all the penalties paid and soft jail time, the venture was very profitable. It openly demonstrated a Wall Street business model of predatory fraud crime for profit. There is no such thing as a bank or financial institution that has not engaged in fraud and corruption. "Sure, everybody does it, right?" Government-owned banks are no exception here either.

1989: US savings and loan fraud.

Six pillars of the US political establishment were implicated in a major loan fraud led by one, Charles Keating. It took more than twelve years for this fraud to be fully revealed and costed. Controversy remains as to whether these establishment "pillars" were dupes or actual supporters. More on that subject later. The important thing here is that this was the largest cash fraud of the twentieth century with only minor consequences for the perpetraitors.

1997: Government collapses due to fraud events.

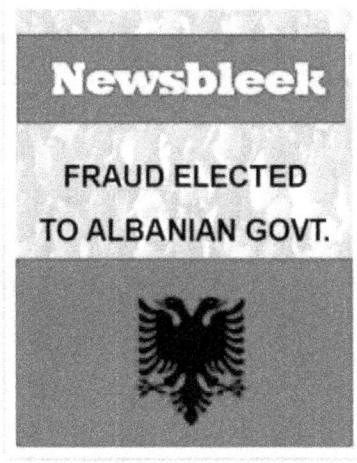

In 1997, the Albanian government was overthrown. This was because of large scale mass frauds raging in the country. Government approved investments. The country had no government or administration and remained in crisis for several weeks. This is not the first time a fraud event has brought a country to its knees.

The unprecedented growth of a global fraud culture.

Blockbuster fraud-focused movies like *The Producers, The Sting, Paper Moon, Wall St, Catch Me If You Can, The Wolf of Wall Street,* and many others have romanticized criminal fraud activities. They have pumped fraud into the heart of media culture as a positive and even a victimless crime. Only crooks and gangsters get dispossessed and their trust betrayed, right?

Thus, we have not only become desensitized about fraud as a crime, we accept it as a normal way to behave. Fraud is so hip now, it's a branch of entertainment. It's integrated into mainstream media with the acceptance of fake news as a reality. There is no doubt that with recent electoral upsets, it is also attacking and successfully undermining financial systems and democracy on a global scale. Fraud is never a victimless crime. It begins and ends with its victims. That's you!

Chapter 12

MASS FRAUD
IN THE TWENTY-FIRST CENTURY

2008: The Madoff family fraud.

This one cost the victims about 30 billion dollars—charities, retirees, and vulnerable people. This was a well-known Wall Street New York fraud for many years before it collapsed. There were seven SEC Investigations over ten years. The failure of these investigations to identify the fraud were touted by the perpetraitors as a badge of legitimacy and endorsement.

This was just one of the countless failures of the highly venal SEC, the US financial services regulator and watchdog. It was an impossible business model. Madoff set up his firm in the '60s and this mass fraud was active for at least forty years. Around 150 financial advisories knowingly fed their investors into it. Less than thirty have been brought to account. Madoff is currently serving a 150-year prison sentence and remains unrepentant, even boastful. Typical recidivist behavior.

2008: The Lehman's Bank collapse.

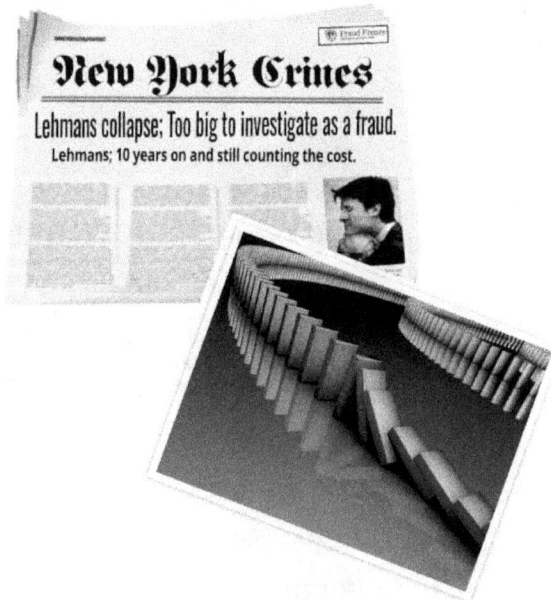

A gushing Fortune magazine described Lehman Brothers as the number one "most admired securities firm" in 2007, just one year before the firm filed for bankruptcy.

This is yet another major Wall Street fraud that was too big to investigate or even be officially declared a fraud. Instead, it was treated as a bankruptcy. This was in 2008 and there were too many huge frauds being exposed at the time. The cost was in the hundreds of billions of dollars.

More frauds go unreported than are reported. This is just the thin end of the wedge, the tip of the iceberg. If you're a victim looking for support or sympathy, you will find it in the dictionary between sugar and syrup.

The Irish banking (cluster) fraud and THREE generations of national debt.

Almost ten years passed before this was acknowledged as a major financial fraud. It came at a cost of hundreds of BILLIONS of euros to at least three generations of Irish taxpayers.

Ah sure, why not fraud?

Chapter 13

ACTIVE AND ONGOING FRAUDS

Deutsche Bank is another example. Their crimes include interest rate fixing, sanctions violations on a global scale, manipulation to control LIBOR, money laundering, etc., etc., etc. They've recently paid penalties and fines of 14 billion dollars to the US government. The estimated number of lawsuits for fraud pending against this particular bank is estimated to be about

10,000. Deutsche Bank, HSBC, The Fed, Barclays, Goldman Sachs, Chase, and Citigroup. Ah, they just all look the same! The all have at least two things in common: a ruthless and relentless immorality and profit by any means.

Here, you will find huge concentrations of mass fraud activities on a global scale. These mass fraud perpetraitors include but not restricted to active pension funds, Wall Street (in the form of your local banks), the US Federal Reserve Bank, and the central banks.

Don't think scheming financial advisers or crooked bankers are anything new. Ever since the Pope (Leo X) legitimized scalable usury through bribery in the sixteenth century, we have forgiven banks times without number for their financial skullduggery. Before this, the idea of any central banking system, like we have now, was anathema. There were epic battles on this front, mostly religious groups versus wealth, all objecting to the corruption and dishonesty usury would bring upon humanity. Looks like they were right. The money won and now they write our history—past, present, and future.

All banks, even government-sponsored central banks exist for one reason only—to create debt. And just in case you didn't already know this, debt is a negative. Many folks actually believe that getting into debt is another way of earning. They market debt as *credit,* and we buy into it. Credit rating sounds positive, but it just represents how much debt you can bury yourself with. A credit card is only a means of getting into (even more) debt. On and on it goes until we stop it.

So, they have successfully changed the meaning of credit. It actually means debt. This is very clever stuff! These are some of the brightest people in the world and they are utterly dedicated to taking your money by any subterfuge. Remember this number: *less than five percent* of fraud crimes are reported. That means these people get ignored. It's not just a free ride but a license to print money; they don't even need a printing press or paper to do it anymore. So, why not fraud?

Chapter 14

Fraud Players
and Their Roles

LESS THAN 20% OF THESE FRAUD SUPPORTERS WERE PROSECUTED.

investment
adviser

broker

In large and long running frauds there are often many players. For example, in the Madoff mass fraud there were at least 150 enablers from around the globe. These were highly respected professional investment advisers and brokers who knew exactly what was going on. In their naked greed, they kept on feeding fresh investors into the scheme, in the delusion their gravy train would chug-chug along forever. Less than twenty percent of these fraud supporters were prosecuted.

Fraud Dupes.

A dupe is often the one who opens a network of contacts for the perpetraitor. This person may have little or no financial value. They are often devastated by their unwitting support of a fraud event. Claims of being a mere dupe is a common refuge for perpetraitors and their enablers after a fraud event.

Fraud Supporters and Enablers.

There are people who openly and knowingly support frauds and use denial or legal shields for protection. Their payoff is usually money and well-hidden too. It's easy money. There was huge cross-party support in the US for the savings & loan scheme until it went beyond bust into the costliest mass fraud event of the twentieth century. These same public reps made a law giving Amway a kickback of hundreds of millions of US dollars. Political support at the expense of all taxpayers. The Panama Papers and more recently the Paradise Papers show the huge support fraudsters also get from our banking systems. On it goes.

The Marks.

These are the victims. Often a perpetraitor will take a long study of the victim or their victim group before they make a move. Victims are usually ignored after a fraud event.

Perpetraitors: the wolves and wolf packs.

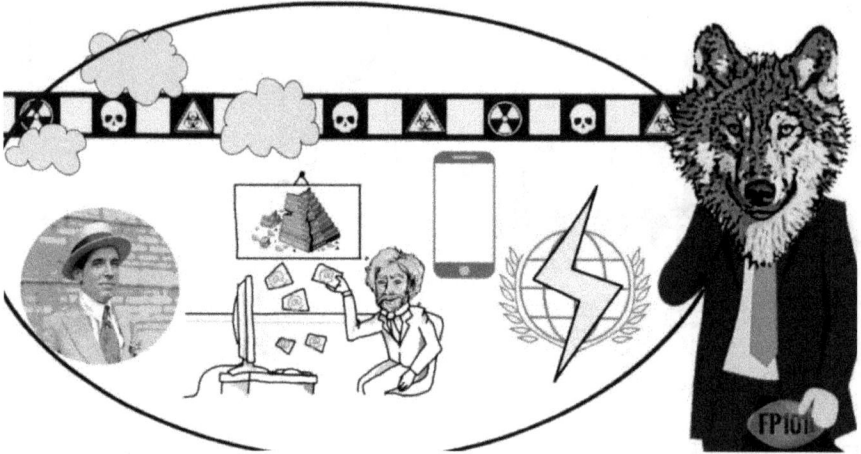

From the street-side, three-card Monte dealer to the fraud boiler rooms, (these are fraud sweatshops) there's a global reach in every major city. From the offer of a "helping hand" to the ever-opaque boardrooms and their mass fraud business models and hidden entities, fraud evolves daily. Something old becomes something new when in reality, there is nothing new under the sun. Wolves wear lambs' clothing—but you already know this.

The fraud line is often clouded and hard to see; you just need to stare it down. From Ponzi to pyramid to chain mail to MLM, then mass communications, then a whole new dimension of fraud—the Internet. Each of these developments has helped to grow fraud levels unimaginably from where it was 100 years ago. Who are these modern wolf packs and how do they function? Let's continue our journey.

Chapter 15

THE MULTI-LEVEL MARKETING (MLM) BUSINESS MODEL

> "There are none so blind as those who will not see. The most deluded people are those who choose to ignore what they already know".
> John Heywood, 1546.

If Ponzi was a wolf, then multi-level marketers are surely the ever-evolving modern day mass fraud wolf packs. Pyramid-based mass fraud/Ponzi-type schemes are an addiction for fraud perpetraitors. Easy money! Indiscriminate but never random. They are like moths to a flame. Led by massive US corporations almost at their ugliest, but not quite. However, these guys are practically everywhere. They are illegal in China and a few other countries.

Few families remain untouched by this open greed, manipulation, and exploitation. In fact, large extended families and whole communities have been decimated by the fake promises and false hopes of these insatiable predators. This is why you really need to know what this fraud is and how it functions. You don't need to understand any fraud or scam to beat it; you just need to know what it looks like. Not only for yourself, but for your family, your tribe, and your community.

The multi-level marketing companies (MLMs) and their disguises.

To fully understand how multi-level marketing (MLM) really works, one needs to be trained or gifted in math. Even then, that may not be enough. That is how this business model was designed. The multi-level marketing business model came out of the original Ponzi-type mass fraud schemes. Product-based "pyramid selling" was around for a while before it exploded out of the US Midwest in the early '60s.

Always controversial, this "direct sales" system has grown vastly in complexity and scale. On one side are the profiteers with billions in revenue at their disposal. They are intolerant of any adverse view or public censure of their methods. A legal army is ready to sue critics, even journalists. Defending itself against governments, judicial probes, and controversy is simply a cost of doing business.

Now that MLM is a well-known stigma, it uses a broad range of other names and guises. "Direct sales" is currently the top preference. Here's an edited list of the names they use instead of multi-level marketing:

Direct sales.

Business opportunity.

Direct selling.

Home-based business.

Concentric marketing.

Referral opportunity.

Affiliate marketing.

Seller-assisted marketing.

Referral marketing.

Consumer marketing.

Consumer direct marketing.

Dual marketing.

Dual-level marketing.

Inline marketing.

On, and on, and on it goes. It's endless. While most of these sales and marketing titles are linked, they use personal network marketing (one-on-one relationships) as their main sales platform. People cannot tell the difference between a genuine opportunity and mass fraud because of all the rhetoric and hoopla that goes into the high-pressure sales methods.

At the core of all these multi-level marketing business plans is an ugly and endless recruitment cycle. They require an infinite supply of distributors and have a high dropout rate. This process is known as *geometric recruitment*. They have devised a fast and highly effective formula. More than adaptive, it's tactile.

This leads to unlimited competition and chaos in its own market. Then saturation. It is precisely why 99.7 percent of people who invest in multi-level marketing schemes lose money. It is covert and complex math and explains why some folks never work it out. They're brainwashed first and may only figure it out after they go broke or sometimes, they never do. Global growth has been so rapid for this reason. New players must be found to feed these schemes. This pyramid-based selling scam now preys on the financially illiterate in over 120 countries.

Multi-level marketers have a big focus on private branded health and wellbeing products. No middlemen. A direct line to its victims, also known as the *silent majority*. A genetically altered mathematical mass fraud system for the twenty-first century. It's worth hundreds of billions to the corporations and billions of dollars in taxes to the enablers—taxes the multi-level marketers are happy to pay and boast loudly about. It creates a full legitimacy within the establishment. Taxpayers are good and upright citizens, right? It is a well-rehearsed and refined mass fraud scheme so toxic and so deeply entrenched, participants have had to be literally deprogrammed to come out of it.

Chapter 16

THE SIZE, SCALE, AND METHODS OF MULTI-LEVEL MARKETING FRAUD

The scale of MLM fraud.

Our main criteria in this handbook is to enable you in becoming fraud aware. We also want to do it without using deep math or geometrics to explain these frauds. However, we can't avoid using numbers to demonstrate the size and scale of it. We are, after all, talking about a specific and global mass fraud enterprise.

Top 100 MLMs - Global

FP101.net

The scale of MLM fraud.

The top 20 of these collectively grossed in excess of $50 billion dollars in 2016.

Amway	$8.80 billion
Avon	$5.70 billion
Herbalife	$4.50 billion
Vorwerk	$4.20 billion
Mary Kay	$3.50 billion
Infinitus	$3.41 billion
Perfect	$3.06 billion
Quanjian	$2.89 billion
Natura	$2.26 billion
Tupperware	$2.210 billion

This graphic shows the 2016 turnover figures of the top 100 "direct selling" companies in the world. Note: these are *their* numbers. In that same year, the top twenty collectively grossed in excess of $50 billion dollars. The total turnover amount for all 100 is well over $60 billion dollars—plus all the billions of wasted working hours. That sure is a lot of thieving.

It's just one area of a legitimized mass fraud systemic. And here's the deuce kicker…the primary focus of these predators is on the uneducated masses—those of us who don't know better. Decent people who simply can't see past their precisely detailed lies and deceits. Poor people who, after getting caught up in a personal fraud, never recover and at best, lose all interest in enterprise and financial independence. Many even lose hope and give up on life. You can even find these MLMs marketing themselves in refugee camps. Sure, why not? There are over sixty million refugees in the world right now. Put simply, you or anyone you know is potential grist for the MLM grinder.

The MLM identifiers: products & branding.

Every 1's a loser!

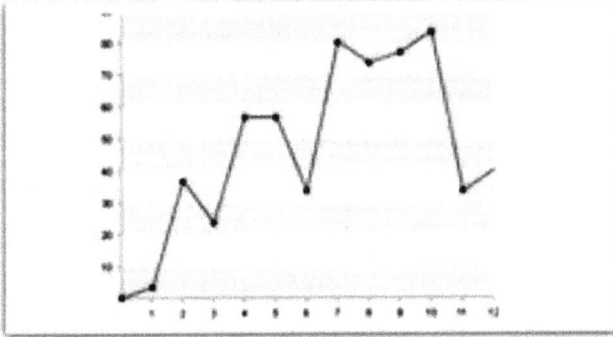

These are carefully sourced and costed. Most multi-level marketers list health and personal items as key products. They're also priced much higher than shops and of disputed quality. It's like the wild west era with Dr. Quack's magic potion that cures all ills. "Only a buck for a bottle" that can be bought elsewhere for ten cents or less. Very few multi-level marketers directly market their products, even online. If they do, it's for transparency purposes. Multi-level marketers are big on this kind of thing. There is an ethics person in every one of those large companies and even a team within the DSA (Direct Selling Association). This is the representative body of the 100 names you see listed here. You probably recognize many of them.

Commission structures.

They have at least four commission structures, each geared to a specific product. Forensic accounting will find these structures a test to figure out. No multi-level marketing company has ever willingly opened their books on their recruitment process or commission structures for any reason. The lawyers have to be beaten back before that happens, if ever.

Commissions can show the difference between direct selling and a product-based pyramid scheme. Most MLMs have five or more commission levels. In a normal sales operation, more than four is untenable. The multi-level marketing level for new distributors is usually a variable. This means that commissions can be slanted towards recruitment over sales. The higher the recruiting incentive, the greater the churn rate. It's a guess at how these numbers are reported in the books. For example, commissions can be reported as sales and vice versa. It's all about legitimizing financial skullduggery.

In order to join and be supported, recruits must buy product. This is often called "pay-to-play." These goods are then "wholesaled" to new distributors who were found by the new recruits. The new recruits then 'wholesale' these goods to new distributors that they find. These distributors are now the newest recruits. Often, the products end up being used by the distributors personally or are given away as free samples. Product discounts, commissions, and bonuses are based on sales to new members.

Many multi-level marketing companies claim the spread of commissions is as high as 75 percent of product sales. Most of this goes to the top of the pyramid. The multi-level marketers with their representatives, the DSA (Direct Selling Association), and their gangs of lawyers insist this is direct selling. This is a legal argument that multi-level marketers have crafted since the '60s for three great reasons:

1. It creates a screen of legitimacy.

2. It builds confusion.

3. It creates a potential legal dispute with any disagreeable interpretation of this business model.

Every multi-level marketing business startup has its legal expert. It's their first hire. If it isn't, they will fail.

The mass fraud (MLM) recruiting pitch.

Multi-level marketing rallies are something special. For energy, good vibes, and exhilaration they are unbeatable. Turnouts of 25,000 or more are typical for these staged events. Their conventions are pitched as motivational and educational. The real agenda is recruitment and consolidation. Unless folks are skilled and grounded, the emotions generated will just blow them away. They get caught up in the moment and make life-changing decisions right there. The pitch is slick, and it works.

"We are the greatest direct sales company in the world!"

"We have seven billion dollars in annual sales!"

"We market our products in over 100 countries!"

"Our products are exclusive and unique!"

"We create financial freedom for all those who join with us!"

"We have 3.5 million sales associates!"

"We have won awards for…everything!"

"This is where your dreams become reality!"

"We are here to support you!"

Each declaration is met with a rousing cheer and growing excitement. Graphics with the statements flash across cleverly placed screens to reinforce the message. This is how the lies and distortions begin. There is no end to it. All they need is folks to listen and they will take it from there.

Chapter 17

Truth and Consequences of Multi-Level Marketing Fraud

The promises and lies.

The multi-level marketing industry owes its success to fudging what pyramid selling really is. This is key in preventing proper legislation and prosecution of certain activities. Here are some of the lies used in multi-level marketing recruitment. For clarity, we will respond briefly to each of these lies:

"This product sells itself."

Even free money won't sell itself. Someone has to make the pitch and people have to believe it. They also have to really believe it is free money.

"MLMs are not a cult."

Then why do families need to get their members de-programmed to get them out of multi-level marketing? Most engage in cult activity and then deny, deny, deny.

"This is so easy; anyone can do it!"

Then why do MLMs have a dropout rate of between 50 and 80 percent in the first year?

"It does not cost anything to participate."

So why do people have to buy things to start and pay to stay in their systems?

"This is an essential and unique product for everyone."

That's why there are thousands of competitors in the same markets with similar products. Usually of better quality and better value.

"These products are very competitively priced."

So why doesn't Tesco, Walmart, Safeway, Aldi or Lidl or any of the major stores stock them?

"These are the most exclusive brands in the world!"

Well, this is why no one you know has heard of them.

"This is a product with the highest quality components."

More lies. MLM products are constantly challenged and prosecuted for poor quality. That's also part of their fraud.

"This is the greatest opportunity you will ever have for financial freedom!"

So how or why do more than 99 percent of people who join actually lose money?

"This kind of direct marketing is the most successful way to sell anything."

Simply not true. Try the Internet.

"Your friends and family will become lifetime customers and thank you for bringing them into this."

They will only thank you if they are looking for an excuse to never speak to you again.

"As a business, it brings flexibility and freedom into your life."

Wrong. It is rigid, demanding, and controlling. It is designed to dominate people's lives until their last breath or last cent.

"This is the number one option for starting your own business."

Wrong. You will be nothing more than a contractor. The business is totally ruled by the product supplier. They insist on COD (cash on delivery) by direct debit. They never give credit. This kills any real cash flow opportunity.

"Multi-level marketing is completely legal."

Wrong. There have been many successful prosecutions against multi-level marketing companies for pyramid selling around the world. There have also been several class action settlements in the USA. MLM is banned in China and several other countries. Paying off politicos is nothing new for corporations.

"This is not multi-level marketing. It's direct selling."

Wrong. The general rule is that 70 percent of all MLM products should be sold directly to consumers. This is rarely, if ever enforced. MLMs are reliant for sales in the recruitment of wholesalers and distributors. It's pyramid selling with product.

Occasionally, the promoters come out for endorsement videos and conventions. They present themselves as housewives, workers, and ordinary people. The MLMs are choosy in showing off these glossy people with their glowing testimonials and grand lifestyles. In reality, these are the top tier of the multi-level marketers—the greedy profiteers.

The MLM cults and cultures.

We all have critical thinking skills. This allows us to make judgement calls and is essential to our decision-making processes. There are books and courses on it. It's a major subject. The essential requirement for becoming a member of a cult is to suspend critical thinking and "go with the flow." That means accepting the ideas of others as valid. No questions asked. Most people won't do it on their own. They need help or persuasion. Call it enablement. This is at the core of how multi-level marketers and many cults recruit. It's part of their culture. Like a drumbeat in the midnight jungle. It whispers. It screams. It seduces. Full of hope and promise for a brighter future. Many are drawn to it. Others become absolutely enthralled and its prisoner. Like a gambling addiction or gold fever.

An utterly abnormal business model.

Most MLMs have a lifestyle focus. Recruits are not strictly self-employed because they cannot set any of the rules. They can also be cut loose for not keeping up with the numbers. They do have some of the benefits of the self-employed, however, such as the ability to set their own hours and decide which markets to work in. But everyone in business needs a little help. There is no support or unions or any other advisors they can turn to for help when it's needed. Instead, they turn to their personal (and professionally inappropriate) multi-level marketing relationship for this. It leaves them exposed to the worst kind of manipulation. *All doubts must be cast aside. Failure comes from lack of effort and commitment. The company is their friend and mentor.* They will believe everything they are told and there is no truth or transparency here.

The MLM rallies.

This is what keeps everybody motivated and excited about the life-changing journey they're on. Seize back control of their own destiny. Take control of their income. What was called a J-O-B, is really a "journey of the broke." A grind. No chance to bloom and grow. It will bury them alive. A job would never allow them to reach their full earning prospects. Never recognize their abilities or accomplishments. Every one of these statements is met with raucous cheers. Every new mediator is an instant idol. When one of the "team" is brought onstage to have their new level announced and declared a hero, the crowd just goes wild. For the believers this is better than going to church.

The MLM playbook.

All the MLM playbooks read the same. Remember the slide explaining the mass fraud cycle earlier? It's the same principle.

Same scheme with a slightly different riff. The riff is that no one can rise above the lower levels except a chosen few. Less than 1 percent—.03 percent, actually.

The playbooks have a few variations for added character and color. Being in business for themselves is just the start. Their friends are also helping others achieve their goals and their dreams. This is why it is so important to bring in family and friends. It is all about investing in and helping others. It's not all about the money and the success.

There is plenty of room here for everyone's dreams to come true. Sure, they must work hard at it. They have to believe in themselves and take the chance to follow their true destiny. Friendship, wealth, and happiness awaits! Ah yes, there are always those who would be dismissive or even critical. People with envy or who are just plain negative. Stuck in their boring and ugly j-o-b and sure, misery loves company. The key to success here is being positive and staying that way. They should no longer leave room in their life for these begrudgers. There are always plenty of those out there. The haters.

The MLM churn.

First, they need to isolate the victim and get a commitment from them. They will criticize all those who disagree with this "new life" opportunity. The dedication is there now. The only place left to go is down. Everybody, except the newly recruited, knows this.

The objective now is to keep them in the cycle for as long as possible. It's their game to lose. In the first year, most of the new recruits will drop out. Some just don't have the necessary staying power or time available. Many aren't comfortable with the morality of this scheme; they feel guilty about the recruitment methods. For others it's pragmatic. They spent about $500 and a couple hundred hours (or more) on the venture and lost money. That was enough. They often leave with regret and sadness that they could not stay in the game a little while longer. These folks are actually the luckier ones.

The MLM endgame—for victims only.

Many multi-level marketing participants will have spouses or partners still living in the real world. A choice often has to be made. Not everybody chooses their relationships. Long-standing friendships disintegrate. Families get neglected. Plenty of angst and tragedy. Life savings get invested. This can run to tens of thousands. Divorces. Suicides. Even murder. Somehow the recruit has become a multi-level marketing addict and changes companies several times. Many people even starve themselves to stay in the game. They visit with friends but are really looking for food.

The endgame for these players is they lose everything they have and end up broken and alone. Most still do not understand why the scheme didn't work for them. Oh! But it is their fault, the MLM promoters will say. They didn't follow directions correctly. They weren't committed enough. These are the last soul-destroying insults.

When you see a mass fraud systemic such as this rolling along and continuously expanding its grip for decades, you will ask how people can treat each other like this. Our answer is that you should not try to understand it. Few folks do. You just need to know what it is. So, be fraud aware!

Chapter 18

THE INTERNET (FRAUD BY A.I.— ARTIFICIAL INTELLIGENCE)

The Internet is a very important and useful tool in our lives. It can be a unifying force for a greater good. Its ability to deliver communications and data at light speed is a gift to all humanity.

This is just one aspect of it. It also has a real dark side. It can only be as good or bad as what we put in it. And there sure is a lot of junk on the Internet. In fact, it's endless which makes it a challenge to get the highest and best use of it with our identity and finances intact. The Internet has become so toxic with fraud crime, users are actually starting to walk away because of this.

Think of the Internet as a different universe. Not parallel or anything. More like an alien universe. We're in denial because it sneaked up on us! Over a couple of decades, it has made itself indispensable to this next generation of humanity. Man and machine in harmony—and denial! If the Internet was somehow recognized as another dimension, even if man-made, then we would use it much more cautiously...and we really should.

At the very least, the Internet as we know it today is the arrival and personification of true A.I. and more importantly, we can already see how it is used to exploit our humanity.

The Internet has three key requirements to thrive and evolve as an artificial intelligence.

These critical needs are:

1. Data and information.
2. Time.
3. Money.

As it evolves, it becomes more creative and smarter at accessing and sustaining these needs. It cannot and will not survive without them. Morality does not come into it. The Internet, like humanity, can and will do whatever is necessary to survive in whatever form it takes. So, it steals and does this really well at all levels. Blatant and brash, colorful and chronic, real subtle and always lurking. Truly a creativity driven predator. Fraud is all these things on the Internet and much more. So now, let's take a harder look at the list from a personal angle.

__*YOUR*__ data and information.

__*YOUR*__ time.

__*YOUR*__ money.

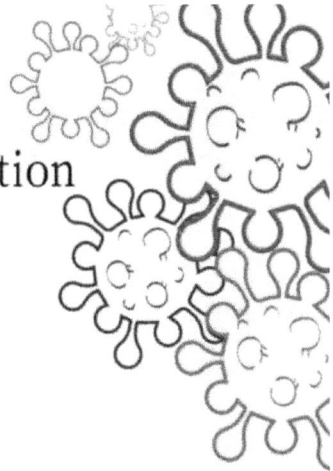

 Data and Information

 Time

 Money

This is what they steal from you. There's just so much of all this to steal! And it never ends. The Internet is a natural home for fraud because all of humanity lives there. It really does bring a new and different reality for everybody, even the nonusers. It is another dimension for our developing humanity to cope with.

Fraud prevention for the Internet: Use it carefully and be fraud aware.

The main Internet frauds.

As already stated, the Internet has become an essential part of our daily lives. In the course of its rapid development and growth, fraud crimes have evolved with equal speed. It is as much a tool for anonymity as it is for consuming data. The Internet is a fraud enabler. It is a gift to the perpetraitors. Nothing can or will change that. You have to proceed with caution without losing the benefit of a great tool. You don't have any choice; you can only use the Internet on that basis.

Here are ten common Internet frauds. However, you will want to stay current on these, especially if you use the Internet regularly. By the time you finish this book, we will have touched on all the prevention tactics for these frauds.

1. Identity theft.
2. Phishing.
3. Email frauds.
4. The Nigerian letter/The "419" advance-fee letter and advance-fee frauds.
5. Lottery frauds.
6. Fake online auctions.
7. Fake jobs and application processes.
8. Education and training.

9. Porn sites—very sophisticated.

10. Freemium games—even more sophisticated.

Chapter 19

IDENTITY (ID) THEFT

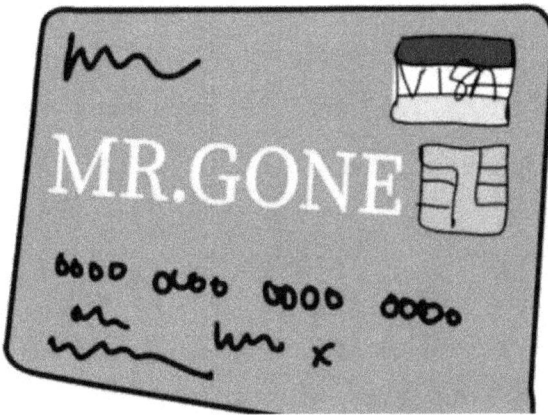

Identity theft and identity fraud refers to all types of fraud crime in which someone wrongfully obtains and deceptively uses another individual's personal data. Even though this has been going on ever since we knew what an identity was, ID theft became a mainstream crime through credit card fraud. No one is safe from it, not even our babies.

ID theft is the fastest growing criminal activity in the world today. The reported losses for 2018 are well over $60 billion and rising. It is one of the easiest of all crimes to commit. It has replaced stealing car stereos and many other petty crimes which has led to a drop in crime rates everywhere due to its low report rate. However, more recently the courts have started passing out serious prison sentences to the perpetraitors. A serious prison sentence can be more than ten years.

People are not aware of the collateral damage until they become the victim. Anyone with an identity is a potential victim. Your personal information is the key element that enables this crime. The only true protection from any ID theft or fraud is prevention.

Identity theft has two main methods: *true name* and *account hijacking*. True name identity theft is where the thief uses personal data to open all kinds of accounts. It might be a credit card account, phone account, access to banking services or access to blank checks, personal loans and on it will go until someone blows the whistle. That's usually the victim. This is a big hole to climb out of, even for professionals.

Account hijacking identity theft is where the perpetraitor uses the stolen data as a means to gain access to the victims live accounts. Usually contact details are switched out of the owners control and the thieves will run up as many bills and obligations as they can before the victim even realizes there is a problem.

The Internet enables the abuse of stolen data because personal interaction is not a requirement for any transaction. There are many uses of personal identity for the purposes of crime. They include but are not limited to the following brief list:

1. Falsification of tax returns by using a stolen Social Security number. This is used for getting illegal tax rebates.

2. Medical identity theft to obtain free medical services. This is usually claimed through health insurance.

3. The theft of a child's identity information. This is where a Social Security number is used to obtain government benefits, open bank accounts, and other services. It's one of fraud favorites because the damage is not detected for a long time—years and even decades.

4. Seniors and aged people are also a favorite target. This is because they are most likely not fraud aware. Due to their regular contact with health care professionals and an easy familiarity with giving out their essential personal data to obtain assistance, they become soft targets.

Identity (ID) theft methods.

Here is a short list of some of the methods they use for one of the ugliest personal fraud crimes.

1. Dumpster diving/rubbish searching. This is about retrieving paperwork and discarded mail from refuse, wherever they can find it. This is still one of the simplest and quickest ways for perpetraitors to obtain essential data about you. So, offers of credit that you have no interest in taking up need to be shredded, as does anything with your name on it. Use a crosscut shredder for this task.

2. Shoulder surfing. Any public venue where people are transacting will do. They will watch and listen for any information from peeking at a form being filled out or eavesdropping on a telephone conversation. Vehicle

registration locations are a classic location for this, but it can happen anywhere.

3. Network hacking and online security breaches. Everybody thinks hacking and online security breaches is where the main ID theft damage is done. This is not true. All info enabling the perpetration of fraud crime usually comes from the victim. You already know this.

ID theft prevention.
Rules and flags for ID theft prevention.

RULES:

- Protect your personal data. Don't willingly share it with anybody.

- Do not engage with spam emails from someone you do not already know.

- Check your bank account regularly for unauthorized withdrawals.

RED FLAGS:

- If bills don't arrive on their due date or any other mail going missing.

- False accounts or charges on a credit report.

- Medical records that show a condition they never had.

- A revenue/tax collector letter saying another tax return was filed unexpectedly.

- Notification of a data breach from a company with access to your personal information.

- Loss or theft of a wallet containing bank cards, driver's license, and other forms of identification.

Dealing with ID theft.

An identity theft confirmation is usually followed by weeks, months, and often years of hassle and heartache. It is not a situation to be taken lightly at any time. Immediately contact a lawyer or an ID restoration service specialist. If you don't have the budget for this, contact all the essential organizations. First, file a police report. Then contact the bank, credit card providers, health insurance provider, and revenue office to inform them of the situation.

Make a note of who you are speaking with and request to have all accounts frozen or closed to prevent any further damage. The victim should also inform the credit bureaus. Ask for a fraud alert and pause on your credit history. It's also a good idea to follow up with all your financial service providers responsible to see what types of assistance and protections they may have in the event of a data breach.

Remember this one thing about identity theft: all the information to enable the theft comes from you! So, protect it.

Chapter 20

EMAIL FRAUD AND PHISHING

Everyone should be familiar with fake emails by now. The best prevention tip for this is to try and restrict the number of emails received. Always remember that your email address has value and by responding to fake emails you are validating this data. If in doubt about any email you receive, verify the info in it before you reply or act. Let's put it another way—if you're going to allow someone into your house, you should at least know who they are.

Emails come in two categories: from *people you know* and *the "others."* So, watch out for the "others!" Never *ever* transact out of an email link. Always use independent access to any website for transaction purposes. It is worth noting that many institutions do not allow sensitive financial information to be transmitted by email or via the Internet.

Phishing is another word devised on the Internet. It is the deceptive practice of sending emails pretending to be from your bank or other trusted brands. The purpose is to get folks to reveal personal data, such as passwords and account numbers. These emails will have links to fake web pages that ask for login information. The top prevention tip is to never click on a link in an email and subsequently use access codes at the destination website. If you are going to access sensitive information online using passwords, set up your own security protocol. Go to these websites through your browsers and not by a click-through method.

Chapter 21

FREEMIUM FRAUD
(AKA FREEMIUMS OR FREEMIUM
GAMES)

*F*reemium is another new Internet buzz-word. An obvious mix of *free* and *premium*. What was considered premium used to cost sixty bucks a pop for the best games. Free because it's the ultimate marketing sound byte. It is a business model that markets online social media-based games as "free of charge" or "free-to-play." However, there are fees for special power-ups, features, or just content.

So "free," the most powerful word in marketing, is used in an open and outright lie. At the very least, this is fraudulent misrepresentation. So, what's new? Not just this, these "free-to-play" games use deep psychology to generate addiction in players from the outset. So, folks who never had any issue quickly develop a very serious problem. This is an addiction that goes way beyond just stealing our time and our money. They also steal our minds and our children—right from under us.

This fraud is beyond scientific, beyond human, and beyond just plain evil. This is about the remote use of A.I. to plunder and steal at will. The click of a button and your money is... gone. Again, you don't have to understand fraud here, you just have to know what it is. And by the way, if you have any doubts about any of this, it is all supported by scientific fact and criminal prosecutions.

The big change in online games came when the wealthy gaming industry moved in around ten years ago. Those people sure know how to monetize fun. After all, that's how they make their money. All the innovative and creative game developers who had any ethics or morals have either moved on or sold out. As a result, we've seen freemium games such as *Candy Crush Saga, Angry Birds, Clash of Clans, Vikings, Dominations, FarmVille* and a huge raft of other mindless and moronic mental exercises disguised as "intelligent" fun and games. It's not even gambling because there's nothing to win. It's all in your mind!

They all operate on the same few basic principles right out of the fraudster's playbook. Designed exclusively to part the masses from their hard-earned cash fast. They take as little as a buck at a time to thousands (called "whales") per player. This is done by creating gambling type addictions where none existed previously. We really do have to use a big word for this. Neurological fraud.

The size and scale of freemium fraud.

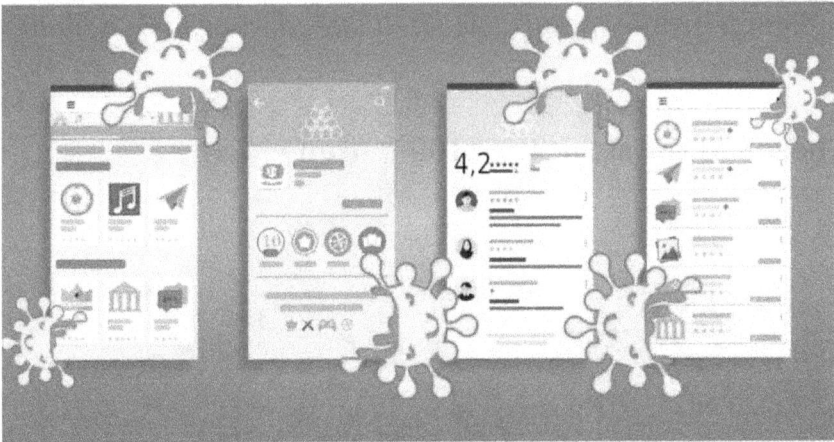

In-app purchases happen in the middle of using a proprietary software product. A button pops up, you simply click on it and then...your money is gone. About 90 percent of the Apple Store income comes from in-app purchases. That's about 5 percent of all app users. However, the big news is that this income is twenty times greater than all other application sales. The in-app sales for 2017 exceeded $50 billion and seems to be growing at a rate of 20 percent per year. Sales through freemium games have become the top source of all mobile app revenues, both on Android and iOS systems. This is enablement and is very profitable for the enablers. It has become a huge industry and those involved are getting very wealthy and powerful really fast.

Most freemium games use a dual-currency system, a type of money that you earn through normal gameplay, and another that has to be purchased with real cash. This big spending is on power-ups or items that aid the player to the next level. Like the drug pushers and dealers, the first few hits are free. Most of these games give nominal "free" currency for completing a mission or moving up a level. It's all part of their addiction strategy.

The art of the steal: the $100 button rip-off.

Super Monster Bros. is a combination of characters from *Super Mario Bros.* and *Pokémon*. It's for young children ages four and up. When it is being downloaded, the adult must provide their account password, thereby giving access to their payment method, a credit or debit card. So, as the child is playing the game, a purchase confirmation comes up, preferably for $100. A child, not fully aware, will click on the button. This is a financial trojan horse and a quick way to max out any credit or debit card. You need to think about this one for a minute before you realize how utterly evil a strategy it is.

Chapter 22

How A.I. Enables Freemium Fraud

Building an income stream off a fraud platform.

In the beginning, it was all fun! Remember *Angry Birds* when it first arrived? Simple, great fun, and almost free. Just a few bucks for lots of fun. All the later versions became freemiums—pay-to-play. They made billions for the makers. The same business model was with *Candy Crush* which pulled in almost $2 billion in its first year and on it goes. Fraud truly is endless.

Gameloft produced *Dungeon Hunter Champions,* which started out as a great online gaming experience. As the game evolved, it became more and more focused on getting at player's money. In the latest version of this hugely popular game, you get the first few power ups free, then it's all pay-to-play. A lot of people go broke on this one.

Take EA's (Electronic Arts) Rock Band as another example. They tried to close that platform down while ignoring the billions that millions of players had already invested. The backlash was so powerful they had to leave the game up. No apology was or is ever likely to be made. After all, this is the corporate world we are dealing with. So, profit before all else, right? And by the way, who are you? And why would you matter?

Freemium fraud: the set-up.

nintendo
disney
xseed
google
sony
ubisoft
campcom
apple
blizzard EA

These games draw in players with very aggressive marketing and social media tactics. Most allow the first few levels to be played for free. Then, a price kicks in for advancing to the next level. There is a key algorithm especially written for the space between a player throwing the device at the nearest wall and putting another few bucks into it. Algorithm is a modular computer code piece written to execute a very specific set of instructions.

What chance do normal folks have against this level of deceit? As you can see, these game developers have not just sold out on their own creative ability, they have sold their souls as well…for about the average price of a cup of coffee.

Even Disney has gotten in on the act. Their game, *Hidden Worlds*, dominated the children's online gaming market. This one is for ages four and up with in-app purchases. In effect, the legacies of Steve Jobs and Walt Disney are being used for the enablement of fraud. What would they say if they were here to see that now? Then again, they were both hardcore profiteers, so we'll never know.

The freemium fraud pathology.

Welcome to the real dark side—deep psychology as it is used to create freemium fraud addiction. The first move is to provide the basic product "free." Then give a limited amount of fast and rewarding gameplay. This really is great fun. Ask any player. This sets up the user. Next is a cheap buy-in deal (starter pack) to get game tools (bigger guns or currency) that allows the user to move forward, accomplish stuff, and get more game rewards. About 5 percent of players spend all the money, often at $50 or $100 at a time. What is it that will get an otherwise smart high achiever to spend this kind of money and with nothing to show for at the end? By the way, the most potent addicts of freemium fraud are the high achievers. Our brightest and best.

These game developers are highly paid corporate contractors. Mercenaries, but certainly not the idealistic version. No great cause here! They're chosen for their great skill, tech savvy, and commitment. This talent is coupled with reams of historical data from millions of players using gaming platforms. The data is then analyzed in deep behavioral studies by professional experts. Plenty of heavy-duty resource investment here and all for a truly sad and dark purpose.

The dopamine effect.

Now, we must talk about dopamine. Most of us just have a vague idea of what it is. This is a chemical generated by neural activity in the brain. Everyone has it. It is a neurotransmitter. When it is triggered, it pumps a deep sense of pleasure into the human psyche. Almost orgasmic. *Oh! What a rush, baby!* Now do you get it? This brain triggered chemical is umbilically linked to stuff like learning, achieving, watching a great movie, discovering new stuff, treasure hunting, being rewarded, or acknowledged even. Winning. It causes addictive behaviors such as gambling, violence, and so on. It's all of the powerful and emotive stuff that makes us human.

These very talented engineers spend all their time finessing new ways of remotely triggering this brain chemical because it will make us do anything to keep the rush going. Throw in a sense of entitlement into this mix and deep addiction might just be the least of our worries.

In summary, these wealthy corporations have figured out a way to remotely trigger an addictive chemical in the human brain and are using this knowledge to engage in the global mass fraud systemic. Like all great frauds it starts with a simple premise: pick a lie, any lie. The lie here is "free," the most powerful word ever used by a savvy marketer. No worries here about being honest, because folks don't see it anymore. Besides, it means little. Nobody cares, or those who do care don't matter. Our silent majority.

Getting people into the game is a calculated investment outlay. Currently estimated at between fifteen and twenty dollars a head in marketing costs. They are looking for one in twenty of those players (a whale) who can afford their addiction. So, the cost of finding a whale is capped at round $400. This is the victim who will "invest" thousands and tens of thousands in the game…and their money's gone. All the other players become cannon fodder for the system. Recruiters even. Bring your family and friends. Remember that one? The only limitation is the time it takes to execute this marketing cycle. There is no education or legislation in any jurisdiction that comes close to stopping this fraud continuing to evolve and explode in our midst.

Gaming addiction.

The gaming addiction.

There are four key steps to freemium game addiction:

1. Lots of free, fun, and highly pleasurable to play at the start.

2. Difficulty and challenges slowly increase to excite and stimulate players.

3. Tools offered to beat challenges and aid progress—at a price.

4. Track the player (whale) and keep it engaged for as long as possible, years preferably.

This all sounds familiar, yes? These games are designed to be simple, yet very attractive. You can drop in and play when you have a few minutes to spare. The carefully designed challenges and rewards are the hook. Researched and created from your data, which is also bought and sold among these corporations. One of the triggers of a dopamine effect is when there is a large and/or unexpected reward during gameplay. It's set randomly, so players never know when it's coming. They do know these huge rewards will pop up if they keep on playing and paying! The dopamine effect does not give them much choice.

The developers have access to so much data on players they can trigger rewards and events when a player slows down or starts to get bored. They're in your head and you don't even know it! There's no law against it either. Yet, we live in hope that even one of our great leaders will wise up and do something about this mass fraud.

If you criticize almost any game online, there will be defenders and a cult following. Even when the game is clearly exploitative junk. Saying they don't buy the in-app purchases is like saying they don't smell it when someone farts. The core design and development of these games is around a cleverly disguised addiction process. Why should drug dealers get all the money? Just because these games are free, and the danger so deeply hidden does not make them any less toxic or fraudulent. Freemium games need to be understood as a clear and present danger to the human condition, especially our children. Plenty of folks already know this, but who's got the vision and courage to act on it?

Freemium fraud summary.

This is about humanity versus advanced artificial intelligence. There is only one winner here. This process is what psychologists term a *variable ratio reinforcement schedule*. This is the same stuff that keeps folks playing slot machines endlessly, the cornerstone of the multi-billion global freemium mass fraud scheme. Compliments of the gaming industry. They pay billions in taxes too. Gaming has government oversight in most developed countries. Sure, even the governments run lotteries! We're alright then. Nothing to worry about. Go back to sleep.

Chapter 23

ADVANCE-FEE AND FAKE AUCTION FRAUDS

The Nigerian "419" letter frauds.

The Nigerian letter fraud is a long-standing scam that has grown into a subculture across the globe. Most of these letters contain offers to become an intermediary for a large reward. Many professionals, especially solicitors and lawyers, fall victim to this fraud, too. It goes back to paying money upfront for something you don't know if you'll get. This comes in all kinds of variations. The best prevention tactic is to make sure you check out a few samples to know what this fraud is and then ignore it. We have already covered advance-fee scams in detail.

Lottery frauds.

Lottery scams are just an Internet variation of advance-fee frauds. There are five main types of Internet lottery scams:

1. A letter, email, or other communication with the joyful news that *you are a winner!*

2. An offer for free entry to play on a website followed by a notice that you have won.

3. Offers of secret strategies or programs that will guarantee a win in a specific lottery.

4. Green card lottery for immigration visas (usually for the USA).

5. Sweepstakes type draws. Not actually a lottery but few know this or care.

Prevention is easy. If you want to use any such gambling products, they are usually government-run or government-licensed. Check them out before you play. Here are a few key ways for avoiding scam lotteries:

A. "You can't win if you're not in." Legally, there is no such thing as free lottery tickets. You have to buy them.

B. You never have to pay any lottery to collect winnings. You pay taxes after you get the money. There are no fees for winning a lottery.

C. If you are fortunate enough to have a winning lottery ticket, you must claim your prize. It's a quick process. They don't normally contact the winners; they keep the money instead.

D. Most countries place a legal bar on foreign lotteries. Plus, local and charity lottery winnings are often tax-free. Some lotteries only pay citizens of the countries where the lottery takes place. The Spanish El Gordo lottery is an example of this.

E. Fraudsters make up names for their sham lotteries, so they aren't listed anywhere officially.

F. If the lottery is not run by a charity or government, it's probably illegal.

So, now you know about lottery fraud. The way to 100 percent avoid this fraud is to avoid gambling. The best way to look at any form of gambling is as expensive entertainment.

Fake (Internet) auctions.

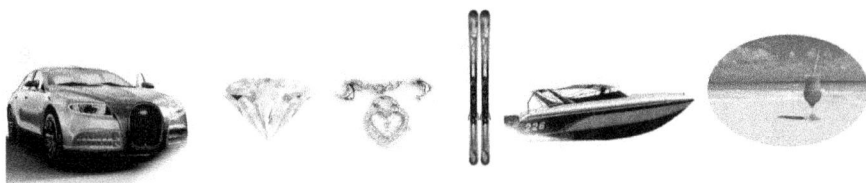

Historically, auctions have been magnets for fraud. Whether it's the crooked auctioneers, vendors, or even the bidders. It gets confusing fast, right? Let's break this down then. But, before we do this, it must be said that the auctioneering and real estate professions are well regulated in the developed world. It's not just about survival and success; they must function properly. A good reputation in this profession is hard earned and much valued (useful to know). Don't let that stop you from running a background check before hiring *any* intermediary and always measure their success by results.

Auction websites.

Let's start with ebay.com. Great fun, right? But—everybody knows that buying stuff on eBay or through any other established online auction site can be risky. It took the eBay owners a while to figure this out when the brand began to fall into deep disrepute. Even years later, despite some stringent policing efforts, there are still plenty of warnings about fraud on eBay. This is not simply a criticism of these online auction websites; just be sure you know what you're getting into before you start buying and selling there.

Payment systems.

Having said that, without eBay, you would not have PayPal. This is one of many payment systems that made its brand supporting legitimate auction sites such as eBay. For whatever reason, it has recently lost its prime position as the payment method of choice for eBay.

PayPal has grown very quickly into a global entity and is now used by many people who don't have easy access to or cannot afford a regular banking service. These guys are highly questionable in their ethics and general conduct. In some areas, they try to present themselves as a full banking service—which they are not. They're buying and selling money now. Financial services with questionable ethics, marketing, and all that.

They have been caught exploiting (and have been heavily penalized for defrauding) their customer base. Simply put, PayPal does not pay much attention to honest business ethics. What's new? Remember the mouse and the peanut butter scenario? Think of *any* financial services provider as the mouse and your cash as the peanut butter. Now you now have it all figured out! In order to steal anything, they have to get access first. Look it all up at www.paypalsucks.com. Then proceed accordingly with *all* of them.

Penny auctions explained.

The Internet is a natural platform for the mechanics of the auction process. There are now thousands of auction websites online. There has also been a huge growth of what are called *penny auctions*. They are unlike a normal high bid auction. Instead, bidders must pay before they bid. Effectively, it's another pay-to-play scam. Often, users must pay to register and then purchase bids. Plenty of hidden costs. For example, it might be fifty bucks for fifty bids. Then, when you start bidding in increments of one penny or one cent, the countdown timer resets and the endgame is the highest bidder who wins when the timer clocks out.

These websites make their money from the bidding not the sales. How does a top of the range smart phone worth $1,000 sell for $45? Easy. At a penny per bid, this represents a total yield of 4,500 bids at a cost to users of $1 per bid. So, they have a margin of about 3,500 bucks on this one item. Easy money and a complete fraud.

The website marketers then push the idea that folks can buy these high-end consumer products for pennies on the dollar. You will even see their advertisements on mainstream T.V. You can't have these mass fraud crimes without such enablers. Often that will be the whole damned village!

The US FTC, Federal Trade Commission, which is supposed to be the consumer watchdog and regulator, has found that on top of all this, some of these auctions are rigged! They use algorithms and shills to boost the bidding thus creating false bidding wars. The FTC has also reported there are many complaints about late shipments, failure to deliver, non specification or non branded products, and so on. So, not only is this auction function itself a fraud, but the entire operations are shrouded in fraudulent misrepresentation through and through.

These websites at best provide very expensive entertainment. Now you know where to go if you want to be defrauded as a certainty. You have a better chance of winning if you go into a casino and put your money on black or red.

Chapter 24

EDUCATIONAL AND TRAINING FRAUD

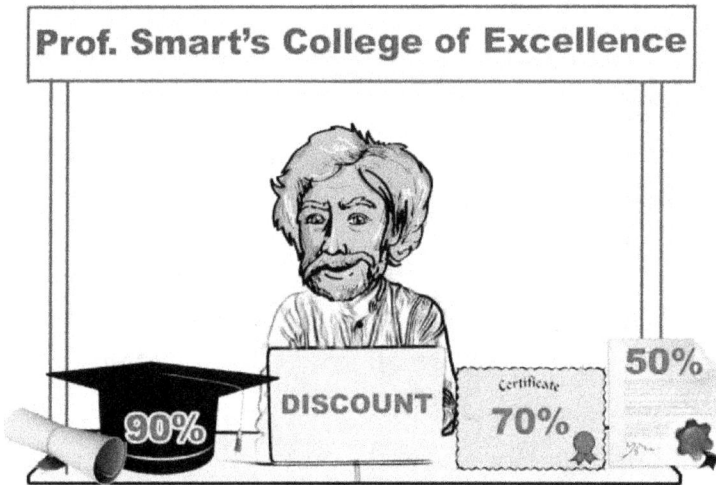

Prof. Smart's College of Excellence

This fraud has been around since the stone age. It comes in many forms. When this scam is leveraged into a massive and institutionalized fraud systemic, the results are most negative. It starts with poor quality tuition and causes immediate and huge damage to careers and life choices. The casualty rate is still growing, so this is a very active fraud that has no boundaries.

You probably have figured this out already. So, let's put it into perspective.

The three dimensions of educational fraud.

1. The mass frauds perpetrated by educational institutions against consumers including students and children.

2. The frauds perpetrated against these same institutions.

3. These frauds are active within the entire education system, public and private.

The whole educational fraud spectrum is huge. Put it in the top three of global mass frauds. Most folks aspire to an education. There are many who use this as an opportunity for both financial and ideological exploitation.

There is little or no public protection against these frauds. The closest thing is taxpayer funded bailouts that now cost billions at a time. Sure, we all know that's nothing more than enablement. Getting educated is not only about money, it's a huge commitment on several counts. Educational fraud is a dramatic example of a collateral damage that is far greater than the material loss.

Here are the key steps for fraud prevention in education.

1. Prepare a formal and balanced education plan.

2. Review in detail the academic quality and financial history of the proposed institutions that will be providing the education.

3. Review the sources and development history of the courses to be taken.

4. Many institutions seek fees annually in advance. Try to mitigate this financial exposure. Negotiate this to a monthly or quarterly payment. Securitize the educational process to protect the student from fraud.

5. Review the examination protocols.

6. Check all licenses and permits and review any history of lawsuits.

7. Have an alternative education provider to use in case the current one turns out to be unsatisfactory.

Finally, learn to value and respect good quality education. It is the shining light of all our humanity.

Fake jobs and (more) training frauds.

Again, this is a variation of the money upfront scam. It has many new forms since the Internet. It might be a strange job offer, a phished LinkedIn or employment page, or emails scrounging for your personal data. It often asks for an upfront prepayment for services. Many students and poor foreign workers find themselves alone and abandoned because of this fraud. It's certainly one of the meanest frauds there is. For some of the victims of these frauds, the only thing they had to their name was a hope they could make their lives better.

Chapter 25

FRAUD AGAINST OUR SENIORS AND AGED

Stalking the most vulnerable.

There are professional fraudsters who have chosen seniors and elderly folk as their prey. These poor folks are usually not fraud aware and are therefore much more vulnerable and exposed. This includes Ponzi and pyramid schemes like the Madoff fraud. People need to understand why the global banking and investment systems are rigged against passive investors. Even freemium frauds have a niche here.

Fraud against the aged is very specific for two reasons. First, it takes someone who is delusional and lacking in conscience or morality to commit these crimes. Second, the scams used are designed especially for the senior-age groups and their frailties. Most jurisdictions have outlawed fiscal abuse of our elderly. However, senior fraud is increasing. It is not so clearly defined in most jurisdictions, so let's call it right now.

Here's a list of some of the approaches fraudster's will use against the elderly.

1. Provide friendship or companionship.

2. Get hired as a personal aide or "carer".

3. Offer therapy services.

4. Provide homemaking services.

5. Pose as a priest or another spiritual role.

6. Profess love to the older person. Also known as the "sweetheart scam."

7. Hang out with seniors and become known as a "charitable" worker.

8. Befriend recently bereaved folks they find through death notices.

9. Pose as telemarketers selling essential elderly and health products.

10. Deliberately damage a property and then offer to make the repairs.

11. Call to the home with fake IDs that create a chance for theft or even a relationship.

The top senior and aged frauds.

1. **Health and healthcare fraud.**

   Such frauds include healthcare and health insurance fraud.

2. **Non-performed services.**

   Fraudsters bill insurers for services that weren't actually rendered by changing bills or submitting fake ones.

3. **Counterfeit drugs.**

   These are mostly sold over the Internet.

4. **Fake homeopathic remedies.**

   Many of these do absolutely nothing for the user.

5. **Telemarketing fraud.**

   Anyone old or living alone is a hot target for swindlers selling bogus products and services across the telephone. Estimates from the Department of Justice show that crooked telemarketers steal, from one in six people, about $40 billion annually in the US alone.

6. **Reverse-mortgage scams.**

   These are very ugly frauds. When the perpetrators are successful and often result in putting the victims on the street with no home to go to. All done legally of course. These are also known as home equity conversion mortgages (HECM).

7. The grandchild in need con.

7. The (fake) Grandchild in Need Con

This is both deadly and devious and when it catches, it runs straight and through like an arrow right to the heart of the victim. It starts with a phone call. It has an almost standard first line, "Hi grandma or grandpa, do you know who this is?" "Becky?" they might respond, thus creating an identity for the caller. Now the fraudster is *in* and will leverage this piece of information into a dialogue led mostly by the grandparent until it ripens into the purpose of the call. They will ask for the money to be sent to a Western Union type of operation that may not even ask for an ID. Then the closer is a plea not to tell anyone because that would get them into a world of trouble with parents or family.

While this may seem like an easy fraud to see through, it has been very successful. It has taken elderly people all over the world for millions.

8. Death and debt.

There are fraudsters who check the obituaries many times a day. When they find a suitable passing, they will call, visit, or attend the funeral service. The objective is to exploit the grieving spouse. Often, they will claim an unpaid debt and try to get cash to settle this fake debt.

There are many variations of this fraud because of the vulnerability and stress of the victims. Some funeral homes and directors can also be very exploitative. Quite a few have been caught at it.

Fraud against our elderly is an endless cycle of criminal resolve and greed. And the only real weapon for seniors is to know what these frauds are. Help them be fraud aware. You too will be a senior someday. We can see it in your future. Now that's ten bucks you owe us, please.

Chapter 26

THE FRAUDSTER'S TOOLKIT

Again, we'll take the perpetraitor perspective. Here's a very specific list of tactics used by fraud perpetraitors. It can be a combination of one or more of these strategies in random order.

1. Empathy.

A key element in human interaction, empathy is the most insidious and pernicious of all the fraud tactics used by perpetraitors. For the fraudster, it's all about building empathy into trust at any opportunity. This will then translate into a deal of some kind and you're in deep before you know it.

Fraudsters will show up just about anywhere. Networking gigs, seminars, charity events, committees, schools, and all social events. Charities and voluntary groups are favorite contact points for them.

Your personal and family life will always be your greatest vulnerability. You should always ask yourself this: is it worth the risk of mixing both personal and business life—especially when your wealth increases and you become more established? Fraudsters, especially the recidivists, see a referral through an existing connection as a golden opportunity. A hot sales lead. Access is everything for them. Your empathy is the key to your psyche and well being. It's who you are and where you live. Always be mindful of this.

2. Bait 'n switch.

This starts with a sweet, simple, straightforward deal. Almost too good to be true. At the very least, you have to look into it. Then at some point, the deal changes into something that is beyond your comfort zone and not as promised in any of the collateral or marketing brochures. We all think we can see this one coming—oh yeah! Then you'll ask yourself how you didn't see it right at the start? Always read changing deal terms as a red flag for fraud. If deals started out as obvious frauds, nobody would be doing them! Don't get caught up in the moment and never sign anything you don't fully understand. Remember your (step) line. Get advice on these major decisions.

If fraud was a shotgun, then bait 'n switch is the load and lock mechanism. Don't forget this.

3. Money upfront.

Money upfront is a fraud that still works very well and in vast numbers. All they need is a good story, slight credibility, and off they go! This one comes at you from almost everywhere: emails, contractors, loan and mortgage brokers, real estate people, even some accountants, and lawyers. There's a lot of folks out there who don't know the difference between a deposit and a retainer. Some reputable companies' business models require a booking deposit. Think of this as a calculated risk and your decision. To avoid this fraud, you must stay ahead of the financial curve.

This means you are never financially exposed. You do not pay for goods or services before delivery without some protection. Professional sellers and service providers already know this, so you will not be the first objector.

4. High return—low risk.

If it sounds too good to be true, it usually is—and you should know this already. These deals usually have little or no security for your investment. High return investment deals are rarely successful. Less risky to go and place your tank on black or red or even the turn of a card…any card.

5. Numbers games.

Numbers is a language some of us struggle with all the time. Many of us have a complete mistrust of them, while others remain mutely loyal. Some of these fraud guys are so good with numbers they can even fool forensic accountants for a while. You will often see this happening after a fraud is revealed. The point of exposure in a fraud is what we call *the reveal*. It is important to know that it is easy to have numbers lie. Numbers are a tool, just like a blade. They can be used with varying degrees of skill to create illusions. So, the numbers games are very commonplace. Bring on the smoke and mirrors!

You deal with numbers like everything else. Keep it to a simple addition and subtraction story that has a beginning, a middle, and a profitable end. If it doesn't add up or make sense, don't waste your time. Move along.

6. Inside info aka "The Greed Play."

Our egos tell us we are quicker, smarter, and smoother than our competitors. This is not often true but our egos drive us and make us naturally competitive in all things. So, when you're hungry for a deal and starving for cash flow, an offer of inside information can be irresistible.

If you decide to engage with such an offer, your diligence must be very thorough. Always remember, using such information for financial advantage is often illegal—depending on the product and the country you're in. This tactic is also used to turn victims away from reporting the fraud after the reveal.

7. Pressure to close. ABC = Always Be Closing.

ABC is all about a high pressure sales pitch. This is a preferred tactic to be used against inexperienced folks. Any salesperson worth a commission knows this one really well. There's a great example of the boiler room sales environment shown in the movie, *Glengarry Glen Ross*. Well worth a look if you have not seen it already.

If you are not allowed the time for a proper diligence, especially in any financial matter, simply walk away and never regret it. Use your (step) line.

Deals can get tough. There is always pressure on the buyer and the seller but these are two entirely different situations. Don't allow one to bleed into the other. And always know which side of a deal you're on. Fence sitters get splinters, don't you know?

8. Foreign and holiday investments.

The amount of people who get into deals in another country and/ or a different legal jurisdiction without considering the logistics of this decision is large. The number of folks who get involved in deals while on vacation is also startling. It happens all the time! Investing outside of your legal jurisdiction is a high-risk strategy. It should be left to professional and local investors. Very few people have the time and money to hop on a plane or hire a lawyer to go fix problems with an investment. Fraudsters know this well and probably better than anyone, so it becomes a tactic.

Any vacation presentation only takes the time the "seller" has to spend with you. After that, other than a few reassuring phone calls, they've got your money...and it's gone. Most of these investments go sideways, usually because of fraud. Should you mix your business and personal life to this extent? Well, if you take a holiday, stay away from the local Kool-Aid, it can be very expensive!

9. The most binding tactic.

All fraudsters leverage one tactic across all their frauds—greed. It is often the prime motivator for most victims involved in a scam in the first place. When the fraud is finally revealed, they feel embarrassed, ashamed, and fearful about their behavior. All part of the plan! Greed and foolishness are like Siamese twins joined at the hip. Dump one of these and the other will follow. So, go ahead and pick!

Chapter 27

PREVENTION 101—ANOTHER 8 KEY STRATEGIES

You don't have to understand fraud to beat it, you just need to know what it looks like, then you'll see it coming.

Preventing a fraud event in your life should not be so difficult. Once you become fraud aware, it's a matter of applying a few basic self-protection rules and then being mindful of its power. You don't have to understand fraud to beat it. Very few folks do. There are as many strategies for fraud prevention as there are fraud crimes. That's the good news! Here are a few moves that you can make for prevention with just a little effort.

1. Protect your data.

banker   lawyer

1.Protect your data.   accountant

SHARE

All the info that enables fraud comes from you! Your DoB, phone number, email address, home address, Social Security number, credit card details and on it goes. This is your key fraud prevention rule. Don't be afraid to ask all recipients of personal information what their rules are for protecting it. You could also ask if they are insured or bonded in the event of a hack or any abuse of your data. At the very least, it might make them stop and think about this; you will, that's for sure. Any information you share with a third party has the potential to be used against you. You need to accept this right now. Bankers for example, are notorious for their treachery and general skullduggery. They are even less trustworthy than lawyers because they don't observe any honor code. All lawyers and solicitors are servants and bound to the courts and legal system. The most trustworthy profession is an accountant, but they are also bound agents for most revenue services; that's the tax collectors.

Develop an attitude about your personal data. You are one of a kind, so it's unique and precious.

2. Stay ahead of the financial curve.

This means don't allow yourself to become financially exposed. In effect, you take the view that once you give anyone money, it's gone. So, if you want to lend money to family or friends, you don't. You just give it and don't expect it back. Paying anyone in advance for any reason is viewed as a high-risk strategy, especially by you. Part of your fraud prevention mindset.

3. Diligence and background checks.

Diligences have to be conducted before making any commitment. If you fail to run a check on someone new coming into your life, you're just asking for trouble. Such are the times we live in. References are good, but a hundred dollars will go a long way in this situation. You'd be astonished what even a cursory check will throw up. Background checks should always be discreet. Act accordingly. Information is power, don't abuse it.

4. In all material matters, especially finance, take a FEE perspective.

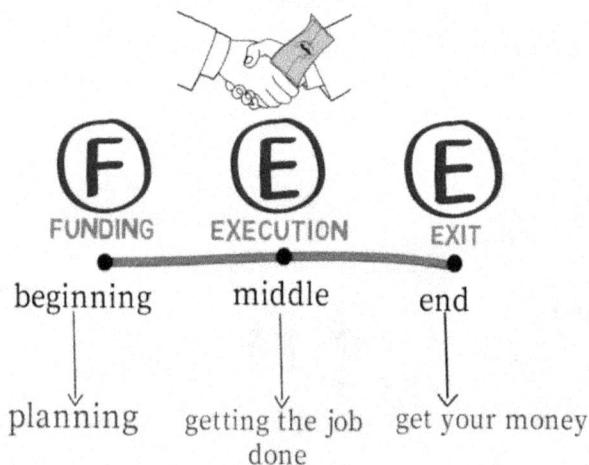

Anything you are going to accept as valid must have three parts. Especially when it comes to material issues. The beginning. The middle. The end. This works particularly well with income and investments. So, with any investment the first part is funding. F is for funding. To get funding, there has to be a plan. E is for execution. This is a learned skill. Execution is about getting the job done. E is also for Exit. This is where you get your money and get out. That's it. Three parts to every deal. Beginning, middle, and end. Funding and planning. Execution. Exit. Think FEE and you'll get it!

5. Understand security.

A lot of folks don't understand what security is and how it is leveraged. Or what is required to maintain it. Ask any lawyer, accountant, or banker (well, maybe not the banker). Knowing how to leverage security is the key to nurturing wealth. You can't have one without the other.

6. Informed decisions.

I have nothing to lose.

If you're going to commit yourself to someone with nothing to lose, know it before you do. Leave your ego out of this. The prisons are full of people who had nothing to lose but their time. Think material triage. It's all part of making an informed decision.

7. Nurture.

This is a constant of review-and-verify, especially with active investments. And it never ends. Don't expect it to. Your wealth will not grow or survive without being nurtured. It's a key element of your material well being. Remember this word and think about it often. Think of nurture one of the biggest words in your dictionary!

8. Do the paperwork.

Paperwork is the enemy of fraud. We've mentioned this a few times already. So, remember your potty training...

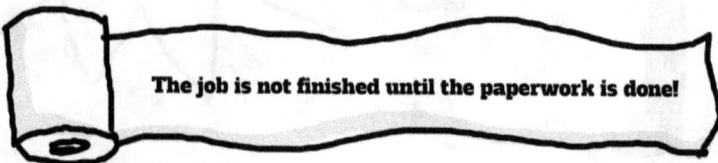

The job is not finished until the paperwork is done!

Chapter 28

DEALING WITH LIES
AND LIARS

"If you live a lie long enough, it becomes my truth" - Dapper Dan

Where the lies are.

It's a fact of life that everyone tells lies—without exception. It is a part of the human condition. At first, we lie to ourselves, even if only for practice. Then the lines blur and we believe it. For a few, the act of lying spirals out of their control, causing them to become habitual liars. When parents or leaders unwittingly lie for a "greater good," many see this as an example to be followed. There are so many who lie for laziness, to ease their way through their days, not realizing the error of their ways. Then there are those who develop darker and stronger motives—money, power, or ego—and thus make a lifetime commitment to it, their morality forever askew.

All that the rest of us can do is aspire to the truth. Let's stop judging someone who we catch in a lie that way we can see a bigger and clearer picture. Truth is not a reality; it is a human aspiration. Deceit is a part of human nature. This goes right back to the survival era. It is beneath the surface in us all. The nearest any human can get to the truth is through a three-dimensional perspective. That's not always a comfy spot either!

The reasons for lying are as varied as the types of lies and liars there are. Denial is the prime reason for why we lie to ourselves. Pride is also a top motive. There's a perceived social benefit to be had by sounding grander than we really are. There's always been a material benefit to lying which has now become acceptable when it comes to doing business. There is also the manipulation game and the need to gain control of a person or any given situation. Fear of criticism and the reality of truth bring us full circle back to denial. So, we lie to ourselves a lot.

The Internet with its extreme levels of bad data has become a haven for habitual liars. Email, social media, and imaging have made lying normal and accepted. Spreading any lie is a rapid and simple process. There are no boundaries. Not print, but multi-click access publication makes it real and acceptable to those who don't know better or think things through.

Deception has become so prevalent it continues to be defined by only two colors. *Black hat* describes the fraudulent application of technology and *white hat* is the truthful version. Describing lies as black or white is nothing new. Lies and deceit were never just those colors, so don't believe it. It's a lie!

Types of lies.

Then of course there are the various ways of telling lies, all as old as time itself. Here's a quick list of the most common lies. You might note a well practiced liar will use several of these lies in any given conversation when it suits them.

1. The white lie—for the greater good.

The white lie is seen as morally tolerable on the basis that it is told for the greater good. Deemed the least offensive lie, this is where many liars get their start. This is also a lie now used to replace an excuse. It is always misread by children who commonly bear witness to it. Children are born into the truth and from an early age know what lies are. We always seem to make sure of that. Then usually by example, we train them to be liars starting with this "white lie."

This lie is also the most deniable and is commonly used to draw others unwittingly into a bad situation.

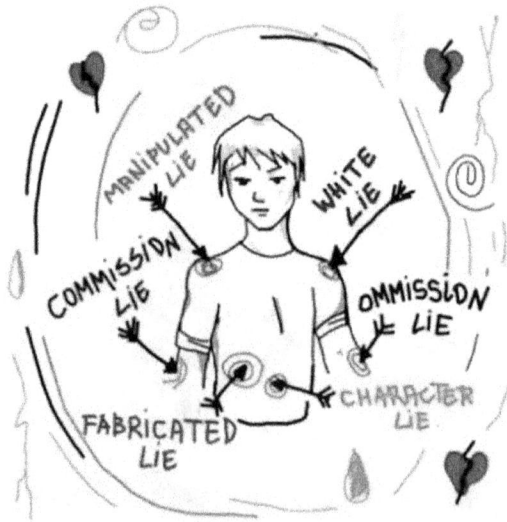

2. Manipulated lie—a lie told by a believer.

The manipulated lie is where a person truly believes they're telling the truth. They have been carefully misled by a third party and are used to spread lies. It's usually very difficult to convince this person their information is wrong. Despite advice from others, they will continue spreading their story. This shows the seductive powers of the manipulators behind such lies.

3. Commission lie—someone who lies for a specific reason.

Also called the contradictory lie, this is the most forceful lie by far. It's at the top of the *liar proficiency* scale and needs skill and practice to tell it. As a calculated lie, it relies on some level of trust from the person being deceived. The liar will leverage any emotion in sight to get any level of acceptance. They will try to allay doubts and fears with promises and assurances that the issue is almost immaterial. This is a lie that often haunts the believer after its exposure. This lie is also used against people with busy lives. Folks going through a crisis and a lot on their minds will easily buy into it. When it looks as if it may not be believed, the practiced liar will switch into a distortion of the facts. This includes clever exaggerations to cloud truth and reality.

This lie often comes just before the disclosure of a larger scheme or an exposure of the deceiver for who they really are.

4. Omission lie—leaving out vital information.

It's very hard to spot this one. A lie by omission is by far the most nebulous and nefarious ways of telling a lie. Leaving out critical information on a selective basis is how this lie is told. It has almost limitless advantages for the deceiver. It is very hard to prove they had the information when they chose to leave it out. There's nothing to contradict. It is non-confrontational. It entails non-delivery of information so there are no tells or emotions involved. It gives the liar distance. Most importantly, it has huge deniability. This lie is most favored by intellectuals, religious figures, diplomats, and media handlers generally. Probably because they can still believe they are truthful people after the lie has been told. Sad to tell, this lie is everywhere. Fortunately, this is a lie that can be countered by diligence and verification.

5. **The character lie (distraction lie, paltering, also known as the devious truth).**

Paltering is using truths or accepted lies to tell or reinforce another lie. The liar tells the truth about something unrelated and uses it as a distraction. This is the preferred lie of those who truly exist in a world of deceit. Like a spider's web with no center. Paltering works so well because it's not a direct or blatant lie. Start with flattery, flummery, and then to empathy which we know leads to the foundations of trust. This lie is very tricky. How can you accuse someone who manipulates the truth for telling lies? For example, you ask someone a direct question and they quickly respond with facts and statistics, all with a spin in their own best interests. The answer to the question might be abstract, but our subconscious reads such responses as answers by association. This lie is favored by politicians, investment banks, corporations, and spin doctors everywhere.

6. **The fabricated lie—rehearsed and practiced.**

Embellished and well-established. The fabricated lie is the most practiced lie. It is a well-crafted and credibly presented fairy story. It comes with another liar's tool, the flat-out denial of any real facts that might be introduced. Whether they believe what they're saying or not, this deceiver will burn themselves in hell to get this lie believed. They are so passionate and fervent; it is difficult to preserve a sense of truth and reality around these ones. They can be just huge!

Our acceptance of lies.

Acceptance of any lie is also enablement. At the heart of most fraud is a forgiven lie. There is a commonality with all liars worth noting. Once they know that their lie is accepted and believed, they will continue to further establish the lie as a reality.

Perhaps there is some way of measuring the morality of a lie? What about the kid with the hilarious excuse, "The dog ate my homework?" Your ashamed friend who says, "I had no idea it was so important to you." Maybe the expectancy is to be told lies as a part of everyday life with reluctant acceptance that this is the way of our world now? Maybe we listen to lies the same way we listen to thunder, waiting for it to pass, barely noticed?

How many of us see the lies and just don't know how to deal with them? Is there a difference between lies? Homework not done or making someone feel better about themselves? Lies to close a legitimate sale or get an investor into a fraudulent deal? Lies to get a war started for a profit?

We need to understand that passivity with liars puts us in their power and at their mercy. Not even a shot fired! Telling lies is a learned and developed skill. It comes from the example of parents and leaders. Lies are also a coping mechanism and even a survival skill. Some of us become completely absorbed into a life of deception.

It is said the truth will always prevail. What if it means pain, anguish, and the acceptance of our own frailty as humans? Lies and liars are everywhere, empowered by those who choose to believe them. It's the softer catch, the snug sleep, a temporary escape from reality. Most of all, lies and deceit are highly profitable when cleverly applied. These lies will only cease when we stop believing them. Telling the truth starts with you not them. They're the others.

Identifying lies.

There are many ways to see lies for what they are. Body language. Eye contact. Mannerisms. There are plenty of tell-tales. Remember, telling lies is usually a learned and well-practiced skill. The indication that someone is lying ranges from a mild ultrasonic ping in your brain to getting slapped on the head by a wet fish or a plank of wood. Listening to lies is like drinking warm water on a hot day. Your first move is to pause for a moment. Do not judge people for it, especially if the relationship means anything to you. Being non-judgmental of liars takes personal discipline, intellect, and even compassion.

Challenge them quietly and privately if you want to get quick results. Ask easy questions you already know the answers to. Engage. Empathize. This will help relax the deceiver while you observe their behavior. Then switch to tougher, unexpected questions. Maybe start at the end of the story and work back. Jump around to various points. Even use abstract questions.

Personal aggression always limits your options here. The liar, subject to their ability, will often give it away by a reaction of some kind. Voice pitch which goes a little higher. Dilated pupils or a slow to fast blink rate as the lie is seemingly accepted. Foot tapping and face touching such as nose, mouth, and ears are also common indicators. Sometimes adjusting or fussing over their immediate space like moving a cup or tidying the desk are also indicators of deceit. Stories are easily rehearsed, but the same is not true of our physical actions and reactions. For specific lying conditions, discuss the details. Be alert for remarks with physical contradictions. If asked a question that needs more than a simple answer, they will often nod one way and speak another.

If the person is known to the interviewer, use a baseline of normal conduct as a starting point of the conversation. Signs might be a cautious calm, a fake smile or emotion, and paleness. Also showing stress in conflict compared to how they behave normally.

Offering too much detail is also a strong signal and can be used to open the conversation. Some people lie for the sheer pleasure of it and it becomes their way of life. Often, this is because it makes them feel better and smarter than those they deceive. There are the habitual liars who always fail to maintain relationships for any length of time. Pathological liars with amazing tales who are utterly convincing. Theirs is an illness which requires medical attention. The key aspect of spotting lies is to know when the truth is being told. A gut instinct that lies are being told is invaluable. It might not be enough. Proving it is better for all. Lying or being lied to is a breach of trust.

There are many who value the belief that others have in them. Then there are the "others" who will readily gamble their integrity in a lie. These others are simply not deserving of any trust. Such philosophy has little relevance in the face of personal financial exposure. An even less confrontational way to challenge a liar is to signal through your words and actions that your world is an honest one and that you act with integrity. You don't understand either the lie or why they are telling it. Who are you to look down your nose at someone who just committed an immoral act you think you never would? What's the point or purpose? Stay focused on facts and not on judging others.

"A man or woman who never made a mistake
never made anything".

People respond much better to a little sympathy. It enables them to be more honest. Try to understand their reasons for doing whatever they are lying about and provide an important and impartial attitude when discussing what caused them to lie. Avoid any "why?" questions. Suggest a few different reasons and they will find it hard to resist putting you straight. The toughest line to take without seeking direct confrontation is to say you don't understand. Repeat this a few times and they'll probably go away.

Handling lies and liars.

Dealing with lies in the context of business and investment matters is a fairly simple task. If someone is found to be deceitful, they must be removed from any position of trust. Right now! If the person has value of some kind, there are plenty of ways of working through this. First, their access to funds or assets or any ability to damage your interests must be neutralized. Think of this as a triage exercise. It is direct loss mitigation and very effective. Their work must be double checked. Failing to do this, the onus for anything bad that follows will rest upon the poor decision to leave them in place. There are ways of handling liars once they have been distanced from a position of influence. If they have no future value, they can be cut loose without any further discussion. They can also be given an opportunity to defend their lie, publicly or privately. There is no luxury of "maybe" in these matters. Carefully consider any decision that will enable any future trust.

Liars are by nature, recidivists.

Fraud is about lying with skill and ethos. All the way to the bank. There are many harsh lessons already learned. Benefit from them. Allowing a deceitful person into a position of trust is more than asking for trouble. Allowing them to go back into place after a discovery of lies is kamikaze stuff. If other investors or partners are involved, this will be seen as gross negligence and beyond. Again, let us be clear about one thing: despite all of this, many of us also aspire to what is true and good.

Lighting the beacons.

Truths are part of our reality and the beacons in our lives.

For every hardcore liar, there are many ordinary people who aspire to truth and integrity. They will not knowingly tell a lie and to do so is repugnant to them. They will take this position as a personal vow whatever their path in life is. Through this aspiration, these people have a consistent level of public trust and the respect of everybody who knows them. Any aspiration to truth will always have its enemies and frenemies too.

These beacons are everywhere. You know who they are if you want to. They may be just casual acquaintances or people you occasionally do business with. A family without this character present will find life very tough. Everyone should have a few friends like this. These people are important because their currency is their aspiration to be truthful in all things. As much as they can be.

Truths are part of our reality and the beacons in our lives. It's never too late to light them up. And watch out for the others.

Chapter 29

THE FRAUD CURVE:
THE NEXT FIVE YEARS

These are most likely the fraud hotspots over the next few years.

Identity theft.

We've hit this topic several times in the book and course lessons. This is and will continue to be a growing danger to us all. Never let your guard down on ID fraud. Ever. It lurks.

Blockchain technology and cryptocurrencies.

This is the new frontier of fraud. The most common fraud strategy is described in *Chapter 8. Mass Fraud 101: The Mass Fraud Cycle (in 8 or less) Steps.* The fundamental prevention tactic here is to know the difference between these two game changers. Just because one arrived on the back of the other does not make them the same thing. One is a blackboard and the other is a piece of very powerful chalk. Two entirely different items. Think of blockchain as the computing language and the cryptocurrencies it creates as the end products. The fraud patterns and methods in Chapter 8 is a useful reference point in seeing how these frauds are structured.

Millennial fraud: freemium fraud.

FREEMIUM

Think of freemium fraud as the true advent of fraud through artificial intelligence. This will become the biggest threat to our society and especially families over the next few years. If it hasn't already, then it will soon pass alcoholism as the addiction of choice for so many. By the time this book comes out, they will probably be calling it something else. Remember all the names they have for multi-level marketing? Same stuff. Fraud is always a variation of the same theme: theft by deception.

Fraud Prevention 101—your one-minute summary.

1. **Think about it.**

   If you want to preserve or nurture your wealth, you cannot avoid fraud prevention as a better way to go. We live in a fraud frenzy and no one is safe.

2. **Know what fraud is.**

   You must know your enemy to beat it. And that means, you must become and stay fraud aware.

3. **Separate trust and money.**

   Use your fraud (step) line for this. Always remember, fraud is a variation of the same theme—theft by deception. At the heart of most personal frauds is a forgiven lie.

AFTERWORD

Let's continue to keep it simple. When you see all this dishonesty and deceit around us, you have to wonder about our human condition. We have to accept that there is a dark side to our humanity and learn to cope with it. Most fraud occurs because of personal greed. Greed and stupidity are joined at the hip, like Siamese twins. There are no justified resentments in this life. Accept that, until we fix it, there are toxic levels of fraud out there. The only way to beat it is to be fraud aware. Education really is the best protection. If this book has helped you with this, then our purpose is served.